POETS AROUND SCOTLAND, IRELAND AND WALES 2000

poetry pt today

POETS AROUND SCOTLAND, IRELAND AND WALES 2000

Edited by Rebecca Mee

First published in Great Britain in 2000 by Poetry
Today, an imprint of
Penhaligon Page Ltd, Remus House, Coltsfoot Drive,
Woodston, Peterborough. PE2 9JX

© Copyright Contributors 1999

All rights reserved. No part of this publication may be
reproduced, stored in a retrieval system, or transmitted
in any form or by any means, without prior permission
from the author(s).

A Catalogue record for this book is available from the
British Library

ISBN 1 862 26539 9

Typesetting and layout, Penhaligon Page Ltd, England.
Printed and bound by Forward Press Ltd, England

Foreword

Poets Around Scotland, Ireland and Wales 2000 is a compilation of poetry, featuring some of our finest poets. This book gives an insight into the essence of modern living and deals with the reality of life today. We think we have created an anthology with a universal appeal.

There are many technical aspects to the writing of poetry and *Poets Around Scotland, Ireland and Wales 2000* contains free verse and examples of more structured work from a wealth of talented poets.

Poetry is a coat of many colours. Today's poets write in a limitless array of styles: traditional rhyming poetry is as alive and kicking today as modern free verse. Language ranges from easily accessible to intricate and elusive.

Poems have a lot to offer in our fast-paced 'instant' world. Reading poems gives us an opportunity to sit back and explore ourselves and the world around us.

Contents

Dundee	P A Kelly	1
The Tree Of Life	Anita Meldrum	2
The Young Depressed	Tony Meaney	3
Ireland, Mother Ireland	Joe Cassidy	4
Interlude	Michael J Murray	5
The Sea	April Uprichard	6
Clans	Rosaleen Clarke	7
Preseli	Norman Royal	8
I Wish	Wendy Blundell	9
The Robin Red Breast	R T Owen	10
Gentility	Gerald Buckland-Evers	11
The Essence Of Scotland	Jean Mackenzie	12
The Fishing Port	Rosemary Reid	13
Silent Music	John E Lindsay	14
Just A Little Verse	Annie McKimmie	15
The Moth	Karen Lawson	16
What Is Love?	L Brown	17
O Rustic Weeping Willow Tree	James Stirrat	18
Oban - Queen Of The Western Shore	Haidee Williams	20
My Parting Shot	Diana Hunt	21
Peace On Earth	Rhys Reese	22
Silver Moon	Justin Anthony Glover-Phillips	23
Milking Time	Martin Hedges	24
Ireland's Hope	Mary G Kane	25
Goodnight Gary Sparrow	Theta Sigma	26
The Comet, 1997	Dawn Lesley Absalom	28
Memories Of A Coal Miner	Alwyn James	29
Ode To The Millennium	B G Metcalfe	30
The Silent Past	J F Grainger	31
The 20th Century	Dennis Stallard	32
The Butterfly	David John Smith	34
Someone You Know?	Lisa A Hopkins	35
Resolutions	Angela George	36
If Your Love Was The Sun	Hazel Houldey	37

The Natural World Around Us	Kenneth E Jinks	38
Mankind	Jeanette Williams	39
He Will Come Again	Deirdre Maria West	40
Shadows Of The Mind	Graham Jones	41
The Pen-y-Banc Brook Near Llandeilo	Laura Föst	42
Islands	Hazel Smith	43
Pontyclûn - Mid Glam	Joan Richardson	44
Looking Forward	Susan M Wilson	46
Believe In The Beast	Martin Richmond	47
Goodbye	John Kelly	48
Shetland Summer	Stella Shepherd	49
Ecstasy	Kay Rowley	50
Glances	Jean Tennent Mitchell	51
Saga Of Two Scottish Cities	Flora Divers	52
The Setting Sun	Dorothy Hill Bradshaw	53
Her Life	Sylvia Mudford	54
Hometown Girl	Valerie Thompson	55
The Seasons	Audrey Parks	56
Magic	Fred W Kroese	57
Fallen Leaves	P H Thomas	58
Misunderstood	Strawberry Fields-Forever	59
Stonehenge	Pamela Evans	60
Endless	Jessica Johnson	61
The Welsh	Kelvin Kriescher	62
Are You Coming Out To Play?	R V Denton	63
Remember Aberfan's Sorrow 1966	Irene Beynon	64
Hearts Content	Mary Hughes	65
A Whispering Wind	R Connor	66
The Wily Fox	C Mogford	67
Dolphins And Whales	Hywel Davies	68
I Can't Forget	Beryl Spanswick	69
Perfect Peace	Sylvia Bryan	70
Alone Again	Megan Guest	71
Another Aberystwyth Sunday	Melanie M Burgess	72
The Mind	Denise Winstone	73
The Last Attack	Celia G Thomas	74

Title	Author	Page
2000, What's Changed?	May Lewis	75
Magical Lovers	Peter John	76
Steam-v-Diesel	Anna Aldridge	77
The Last Rebels Of Change	Chris McParland	78
Rain	Heather Aguis	79
Missing	Glyn Mann	80
The Reluctant Patriot	Sarah Blackmore	81
A Rainbow Of Thoughts	Cherry Eccles	82
Wedding Day	Gwyneth E Scott	83
If I Could	Kim Fry	84
My Mother's Day	A C Dunsmore	85
The Dual City Of Swansea	Andrew Smith	86
Cold Mornings	Laura Smith	87
Cardiff Bay	Tim Raikes	88
Hope	J Mary Dobbinson	89
Houses	Aileen Mathieson	90
Dignity	B Symons	91
Silent Little Children Sleep	L M Scott	92
Professionalism	T H P Anderson	93
Sanctum	Hannah Hepburn	94
Waterfoot In The Shadow - New Year	Heulwen Carrier	95
The Millennium	Elizabeth Greig	96
It Was Only The Beginning	Ann Anderson	97
Untitled	Lorraine Swan	98
Dark Skies	Richard C Scott	99
Trapped In The System	Mary Smith	100
So Like A Dream	Mabel Helen Underwood	101
The Future	Jean McVicar	102
The Cat	Maureen Stuart	103
Committed	Katherine Sharkey	104
Thurso Bay	Christine Farquhar	105
Come	Marlene Robbins	106
The House	Eleanor Hamilton	108
To Clair Gallaher	Janette Rankin	110
Remember	Eileen Parker	111
Old Coaching Inn	John Bonnar	112
Daddy	Myra Walker	113

A Peaceful Nicht?	Joyce Melville	114
This Day, I Make	Baria Palka	115
Farewell My Dear Scotland	Norrie Sinclair	116
The Window	Mabel Nickholds	118
A Welsh Heart	T B Smith	119
Once I Remembered	Gwyne Carnell	120
True Love	Irene Doris Radford	121
Temptation	John Evans	122
Spring Offensive	Norman Bissett	123
Night Skies	Elizabeth Gwilliam	124
This Cruel Place	Maurice Cardwell	125
Star	Damian Begley	126
No Going Back	John Leitch	127
Harshlands	Ken Watson	128
Kolinka	S M Thompson	129
Dragon Tale	Sarah A P Gallagher	130
A New Age Dawning	Ann Slevin	131
The Colour Of Despair	Tanya Fowles	132
Belfast	Karina Dingerkus	133
Tobacco	Lesley P Rainey	134
Winged Blue	Peggy F Haugh	135
My Homeland	Eleanor Scott	136
The Dark	Nicola Pym	137
The Cutter	Calum Cumming	138
My Scotia	John H D Robertson	140
A Millennium View	Sheila M MacMillan	141
Millennium	Gladys Emily	142
Nana	Lynne Bissett	143
Mark Of Decay	Ian Nelson	144
An Egg-Less Breakfast	D L Ritchie	145
Invasion Force	Thom Nairn	146
No One	Wendy Young	147
A True Freen	Fiona Harvie	148
About You	Thomas Cunningham	149
Misplaced Descendants	Colin Vance	150
My Dream	Jeanie Sterritt	152
Fort Augustus Abbey, Scotland	Avril Ann Weryk	153
Millennium 2000	Marion Gray	154

Match Day	Jacquie Williams	156
Early Morning	Lex Coghill	158
Too Late	Eileen P Dunn	159
A Country Childhood	Sara Huey	160
Lincolnshire Reveries	L J Harries	161
Childhood Days	Evelyne A McMaster	162
Scotland	Ivy Burns	163
Teenage Memories	S T Jennings	164
The Sixteen Angels of Dunblane	Ian L Fyfe	165
Untitled	James Callaghan	166
A Childhood Summer	James (Hamish) Seton	167
Never Say My Dancing Days Are Done	Margaret M Osoba	168
My Guilt Is Hurt Enough!	Mike Morrison	169
The Folk Weekend	Paul Keegan	170
The Uninvited Guest	J Henderson Lightbody	171
Someone Sings The Blues	Jules A Riley	172
Today	W Barrett	173
Untitled	Rita Rae	174
Dissolution	Greta Carty	175
Love	Kirsty Keane	176
Life	Marguerita J Johnstone	177
The Artist's Brush	Elizabeth C Craig	178
Michaelmas Bucolic	Alasdair Maciver	179
Pharoah's Wife	Ken Angus	180
Camp 1950	William Easton	181

Dundee

It began with a phone call in mid September,
I think you best come now, the voice said to me,
So I picked up my suitcase and started my journey,
To see what awaited me there in Dundee.

I made quite good time, on my journey northward,
The roadsign directions I hardly could see,
But I hurried on, on my flight of mercy,
To be where I'm needed, up there in Dundee.

So here's to that lassie, my daughter, my eldest,
And here's to her husband who telephoned me,
And asked me to join in the birth of my grandchild,
A journey well worth it, the road to Dundee.

P A Kelly

The Tree Of Life

The roots of the tree forged deep in the earth
Reach down and drink from
The timeless motioning of the planet
Sensing the throbbing pulsations of the world
That give birth and breath life
Into all creation.

The trunk of the tree stands straight and tall
Upholding the canopy
Supporting her incipient life and vitality
Sensing the motion of the wind and stars
That draw energy to the source
Of life itself.

The branches of the tree reach out into the air
And tease the sun's rays
Tapping fire and energy and
Sensing the totality of the universe
The endless striving against entropy
The chaos of the void.

The leaves of the tree soften and caress
The earth and air
Feeding and nurturing, suckling the newborn
Sensing the rainfall, the moment of creation
And enfolding the infant life
Against the eternal night.

Anita Meldrum

The Young Depressed

How few understand them
the young depressed
on the threshold of life
yet sore distressed.

I have watched them with sadness
afar and anear
and never been able
to unravel their fear.

I wish I possessed
two Christlike hands
to set them free
from constricting bands.

Tony Meaney

Ireland Mother Ireland

Ireland
Known for centuries
as the land
of 'Saints and Scholars'.

Armagh
'Ard Macha' in the Gaelic
County of my birth.
Where St Patrick
founded his first church.
Up until recently
the target for many
terrorist explosions.

Drumcree
A quiet country church
where I laid my dear Mother
to rest, years ago
in a plot
beside her parents.
Now a symbol
of division
and a stumbling-block
to peace.

Dear God,
where did it all go wrong?

    Joe Cassidy

Interlude

Each night
in my sleeping,
I hold you
again,
each dawn
in my waking,
I miss you
and
then,
through every lonely moment
of every passing week,
you are
the song within me,
the only name
I speak,
but
when
the breath of springtime,
renews
another year,
it's then
I place a snowdrop,
beneath
each fallen tear.

Michael J Murray

The Sea

The deep blue sea stretching for miles,
Children playing in the sand and making piles.
The noise of the seagulls swooping down for their catch of the day,
The fishermen making their catches miles away.

The noise of the sea as its waves hit the shore,
Visiting your favourite spot as you've done so many years before.
The sea breeze catches you and takes your breath away
Many times you sit and remember and so often think of yesterday.

The deep blue sea with all its mysteries that was once before,
Young children laughing and collecting shells up from the shore.
A young child with his kite in mid air,
Sunday School children running and playing and not having a care.

Young children getting a donkey ride,
Everyone feeling better for their day by the seaside.
It can be so fierce and strong,
And almost anything can go wrong.

Yet it can be so gentle and pleasant and calm to see,
That wonderful enchanting mysterious deep blue sea.

April Uprichard

Clans

Committee butterflies gather in seasoned cracks,
And rush hour bumble bees find substance
in crowded places.
But poppies scatter, germinating in side streets
Coffee their source of fuel.

Weeds are different, like wandering minstrels
they have no fixed abode.
Existing in low dark taverns
or in lonely garrets,
producing dandelions that are time's puff balls.

All seem equal in the pulsating neon lights
reflecting as rainbow pinheads on slimy streets.
But the master magician behind the scenes,
knows they are all puppets being pulled by a string.

Rosaleen Clarke

Preseli

Hush!
Sleeping giants,
Do not disturb them.
See them settled
In sun's last hourglass?
Purple mountains,
Snuggled in close
Under wraps of velvet feathered harmony,
From too much
Overlapping morning time's sea.
Are you ready now,
For the moon's eye call of caves
Or the kestrel's cry of discovery?
As gently stirs the rain breeze
From a late October,
To touch them.

Norman Royal

I Wish

She leaps with feline grace
to sit upon his knee,
green eyes triumphant
as his hands gently caress her silken body,
I watch with envy
as his long strong fingers
glide across her back.
She lies there purring
on his lap,
Oh how I wish
I was that cat.

Wendy Blundell

The Robin Red Breast

The Robin with its red breast
Looking for worms and grubs, there is no rest
When a person digging the garden
The Robin is never far away, with beak laden
Oh, Robin Red Breast, you are so sweet

Watching and waiting while the garden is dug
He is a friendly little chap, he never runs out of luck
He is extra busy when he has to feed its chicks
When they are hungry waiting to be fed, with open beaks
Oh, Robin Red Breast, you are so cheeky

The cheerful song of friendly Robin, brightens up the day
The Robin's dainty optimistic song, I love it all the way
I love the sound of its song reaching my ear
The lovely bird is with us all through the year
Oh, Robin Red Breast, how well you can sing

He gave me a snatch of song this morning
He was a smooth and sleek little fellow, I heard it without warning
I saw him perched on top of a post, having a good look round
I saw him look at me, he was standing on the ground
Oh, Robin Red Breast, you are a cunning old fellow

I must not forget Robin's mate, the hen
She has to lay eggs, which she sits on
And when they are hatched, they in time are ready to fly
The Robin will go on living and fly ever so high
Go on Little Robin Red Breast and sing to your hearts content

R T Owen

Gentility

We all do crave gentility,
All else must seem futility!
For all thought is tender,
Irrespective of the gender!

Those broken words that we hear,
Are only there because of fear.
So all may happy join together,
Really we're just like a feather,

It's not really brave to impose,
More in kindness then may doze!
Thus all may share of God's wisdom,
And make this World more like His kingdom.

That bird that tender feeds it's chicks,
Or fondling kitten mother pricks.
They all do show the truth of nature,
Like that cow in such lush pasture.

Just to be a part of such beauty,
To preserve, it is our duty!
Then we are at peace with God,
Like tired workmen homeward plod.

When we sit back and drink mulled ale,
All of nature we daren't fail.
Each must be grateful for his part,
And to all friends he must impart.

Gerald Buckland-Evers

The Essence Of Scotland

Dark and forbidding is the water deep
Where snow trickles down from the hillside steep,
And swirling mists cast an eerie shroud
As the mountain peak wears a mantle of cloud.
At the foot of the hills in the shade of the rock
Lies an inland lake, a Scottish loch.
Wild and exciting the mountains and glens
What'er lies before, where the river bends.
Waterfalls crash over rocky ravine
Roadside azaleas are burnt tangerine,
The wind whistles loudly - a sad lament
Thro' gnarled old trees that are blackened and bent,
Howling its way with a powerful force
O'er hillsides and waysides chequered with gorse.
As red deer in forests roam wild and free
The essence of Scotland - haunts my memory.

Jean Mackenzie

The Fishing Port

They stand by the shoreline:
Waiting,
Silent sentinels of hope.
Dry eyes clouded with fear, despair.
Knuckles white with tension.
Whose man?
Whose son?
Whose sweetheart?
The cutter lands,
Bodies are brought ashore.
The missing are - just that - missing.
Hope dies.
The waiting is over.

Rosemary Reid

Silent Music

Snowflakes from the sky were drifting to the ground
as you took me by the hand in silence most profound,
then we walked together into a moonlit fairyland.

The tingle on the skin from the crispness in the air,
the warmth of tight clasped hands, that made us so aware.

From the sparkling diamond mantle that covered all around
came the soft crisp sound from our footsteps on the ground.

Words were not required, our thoughts were so in tune as
we wandered hand in hand through that Crystal wonderland.

This is one such story that makes lasting memories.

John E Lindsay

Just A Little Verse

Just a little verse to say,
Good luck go with you all the way,
May all your friends be staunch and true,
In times of trouble to see you through,
Good health and happiness prevail,
As through life's ocean you must sail,
But there is always room for hope,
As God gives strength with which to cope,
To help you face another day,
Despite the trials which come your way.

Annie McKimmie

The Moth

The spider lays waiting, his web is complete,
He's extremely hungry and in need of a feed,
One tug of the web and something's caught,
A helpless moth trapped in a knot,
The powdery wings flutter and then stop,
He pauses to reconsider his plot,
The spider descends his silky domain,
Eight legs crawling, ready for a game,
The victim senses a presence nearby,
Trapped, he lets out a silent cry,
The sticky rope proves too strong,
Death is inevitable, it won't be long,
The smell of fear looms over the lair,
The shadow of the spider fills the air,
The moth jerks and by chance the web splits,
He falls to the ground, not caring what he hits,
A second chance has set him free,
And he sails away into the nearest tree,
The eight legged creature wastes no time,
The web's been mended and he's ready to dine.

Karen Lawson

What Is Love?

I used to go to 'The Plaza' Friday nights
When I was young, and life was still to come:
Above 'Jones' Motor Salon' lay the floor
Where dancing was the start of something new,
And 'Kathy and the Kentones' played the tune.
(It's now a 'Safeway' store, but there's a plaque)

The mating place; time-honoured rites began,
And nascent love excited and inflamed,
Then sometimes died. But on one magic night
Your true love came, and all your life was mapped
For marriage, having kids - then being alone.
(That's life condensed, biology fulfilled)

This Friday night I'm going to *The Vet*
With troubled cat, in kindly neighbour's car;
My pet is ill and I am most upset.
The years between my mating and my fate
Have fled, and left me only with 'herself'.
(But I still dance, since she's alright, thank God!)

L Brown

O' Rustic Weeping Willow Tree

O' rustic weeping willow tree, could you maybe spend some time
                                                          with me,
Do you recall when last we met, there was someone I could not
                                                           forget,
With heavy heart here on my own, I said you'd never weep alone,
Together we both stood and cried, now I've come to say my tears
                                                         have dried

O' rustic weeping willow tree, you no longer have to weep for me,
For the broken heart I had before, it is not broken anymore,
It's filled with love and beats so strong, for with someone else it does
                                                         belong,
And although there's times we are apart, she's forever there within
                                                       my heart

O' rustic weeping willow tree, her thoughts forever are with me,
She's the golden ray from the sun so bright, and the silver in the stars
                                                       at night,
And the beauty I see in her eyes, compares with rainbows in the skies,
And as each and every day goes past, I love her much more than the
                                                           last

O' rustic weeping willow tree, I'm as happy as any man could be,
There is nobody who could understand, the joy I feel when she holds
                                                       my hand,
Or the warmth I feel when I kiss her lips, or the gentle touch of her
                                                       fingertips,
And the joy of knowing she's sincere, when she says she's happiest
                                                    when I'm near

O' rustic weeping willow tree, I've always known where you would be,
We'll return some day to stroll this park, and to carve our initials in your bark,
But we'll wait until we both are one, and we'll introduce you to our son,
And as you look down upon us three, you'll know you'll never weep for me.

James Stirrat

Oban - Queen Of The Western Shore

Oban, Queen of the western shore,
Jewelled Hebrides at your door.
McCabe's Tower your lofty crown
Stands on the hill above your town.
While in your harbour, swelling, deep,
Kerrera guards you while you sleep.
Behind you, mountains cold and high
Where golden eagles wheel and fly.
About your feet are rocks and sand
Where grey waves come to kiss your hand.
At your court in the summer sun
You welcome tourists having fun.
Ferries arrive and turn about,
While fishing boats chug in and out.
You're happy then upon your throne,
But when they've gone, and you're alone,
The Lord of the Sea in chariot white
Comes to your door at dead of night,
Screaming with rage in wind and storm
Until the coming of the dawn.
After he sails away at last
You find the wintertime has passed,
And, in your cape of scanty trees,
Watch how the last of winter flees
From the warmth of your Champion, Spring,
As tiny birds like heralds sing -
Never has there ever been
A fairer one than you - Oh! Queen!

Haidee Williams

My Parting Shot

Yours is the shadow that haunts this smile,
A sad lost melody.
Mine is the anger for letting Love slip
Through these fingers too easily.

Ours is the path which forked in two,
Saw Choice send us separate ways -
So forget flowers, darling . . . just play play Russian Roulette,
Till Fate doth dis-urn . . . with *her* vase.

Diana Hunt

Peace On Earth

Have you ever considered, asked the old red fox,
    The number of inches, wordwide, of rainfalls?
        Of course, replied the tawny old bird,
It is because we are wise, we are owls.

Have you, red fox, ever counted the rivers,
    That flow into the ocean so deep and cool?
        Yes, I have, replied the sly old fox.
So why is the sea never full?

Why do books never exhaust words, old owl,
    Considering the number written and bought?
        I will answer that, red fox, by asking this:-
Why do words never, ever, consume all thought?

I do not understand your answer old bird,
    Nor why you hoot and hoot until night is done.
        Why not fly down here and play with me,
We could then have lots and lots of fun.

The wise old owl winked down at the fox,
    His eyes changed colour, grew large and rotund.
        Why have you and men so many schemes,
When the Good Lord has only one?

Rhys Reese

Silver Moon

Silver moon with hidden strings,
    hangs silent in a velvet sky.
        Morning is a time to run,
            when society rejects my life.
                The usual suspects seem to be,
                      sarcasm and hostility.

That cage my passion burn my soul
    and so for now I'll try to hold
        onto my heart.

I won't conform,
    and so they jeer me.
I'm not the norm,
    and so they fear me.
They try to analyse my mind
    then walk and leave my heart behind.

To reassemble fragile threads.
    I am not beaten.
    I am not led.
    To change my path.
    To change my ways.
I'll be this way til dying days.

So instead of questioning me why?
    Just walk on,
        While I sit and,
            smile.

Justin Anthony Glover-Phillips

Milking Time

Out of the autumn mist the rocking shapes appear,
Sliff-sluffing hooves across unyielding stone,
Ruminating on the day's events.
A gentle sighing sound as full udders sway
And wafts of hay-breath drift up to end of day.

There is a touch of comedy in things
So unwieldy, so serious -
Long-lashed, come-hither eyes
Turned with baleful air to stare
At that strange creature sitting there.

Into the parlour they sway their way
To settle in their private milking bay,
Adjust themselves, legs slightly spread,
And wait for a mechanical hand
To make its soft sucking demand.

No more the cap-skewed head
Nestling into welcoming warm flank,
Rough hands teat-teasing out the stream,
Frothing into the pail below
In steady, steamy creaming flow.

Instead a panting machine
Click-chuffs its greedy suckers
And draws out in impersonal breaths
Its cardboard cartonsful of to-be-skimmed
The result of nature fully trimmed

Martin Hedges

Ireland's Hope

Sad Irish eyes are weeping,
On a lovely morn in Spring,
There's no lilt in Irish laughter,
And the angels cease to sing.

How can their hearts be happy,
When their world is dark and grey,
Irish eyes remain unsmiling,
Until peace is restored some day.

When Irish hearts are fearful,
Longing for security,
And when Irish eyes are tearful
And no hope there seems to be.

With guns and bombs exploding,
Sure the conflict carries on,
Hearts are filled with strange foreboding,
And their loved ones dead and gone.

We'll say a prayer for Ireland,
That her conflict soon shall cease,
Only Christ can dry her eyes and,
Grant her 'His' perfect peace.

Mary G Kane

Goodnight Gary Sparrow

Goodnight Gary Sparrow.
Gone is the bittersweet taste of tomorrow.
Left in 1945 and Yvonne in 1999.
The choosing wasn't inclined.
Left with Phoebe and Michael.
Ron is left to tell all.
Yvonne stands at the gate.
But Gary realises it's too late.
Reg is drunk to hear Gary.
On how his future will be.
His fate saved for Atlee.
It's time for honesty.
(Goodnight Sweetheart)

Scutter Bob

Scutter Bob.
In Red Dwarf, he does his job.
Lister awaits with glee.
As Bob arrive with tea.
Rimmer can only look.
As he takes a leaf of Dave's book.
(Red Dwarf 8:Pete 1+2)

Who Is Kenny?

Who is Kenny McCormick?
And what makes him tick?
The grim reaper can't keep away.
Whatever Kyle or Stan may say.
Eric is on his own.
With self morals grown.
Whatever the cause of death.
His friends state in a breath.
'Oh my God, they've killed Kenny! You bastards!'
His daily rise is a constant surprise.
Unless something hits him between the eyes.
(South Park)

Theta Sigma

The Comet, 1997

The Comet 1997, a peculiar wormhole in the sky
Looked at in wonder, held in awe with a sigh
Keep checking, just to make sure it is *really* real
Yes, high in the sky, I was told, reach out and you'll feel.

The first time I was aware of its showing
I looked out expectantly, my whole being knowing
That I would behold a sight truly amazing
Then noting the mountain obstructing, expectations now fading.

Everyone now had seen this wondrous sight
Except little me, but I *had* seen its light!!
I couldn't move the mountain that was blocking my view
But, *please*, I really needed to see the Comet too.

So I waited and fretted and tried haplessly to forget
About this historical happening that I hadn't yet met
Then quite amazingly before my eyes, around seven
I was treated to the sight of the peephole to Heaven.

It was like a great telescope in the sky, prying
Like a mirror to lost loved ones and friends, caught spying
On the lives of their precious living kin, in the dark night
Blowing kisses and whispering 'See you later. God Bless. Goodnight.'

Dawn Lesley Absalom

Memories Of A Coal Miner
(Bath time)

Many years ago it was,
when I was just a kid.
I remember father coming home,
with tales of what he did.

His face was black as ebony,
his hands not very clean.
His clothes caused clouds of dust to rise,
I knew where he had been.

The metal bath upon the hearth,
before the roaring fire.
Mothering boiling lots of water,
my dad was looking tired.

Every day to work he went,
down that ghastly hole.
Digging at the fallen rocks,
and loading tons of coal.

One day whilst he was bathing,
he turned to me and said.
This life is not for you my son,
to school and be well read.

Those words I have remembered,
wherever I have been.
I made a vow that very day,
I'd keep my body clean.

Alwyn James

Ode To The Millennium

Two thousand years ago they say,
A child was born to point the way,
A light to show us man's true worth.
To live in harmony on earth.
And yet today strife still goes on
Man's fear and greed is still as strong,
Mankind is small and nature vast,
And what can stand against her blast.
And yet we joust with her and pay.
Pollution we can't clean away.
So let us party, full of cheer.
But this is not just any year.
Our resolutions must be plain.
We must not tolerate the pain
Of people crying out their claim.
The young, the weak, the halt, the lame,
So fill your glass with sparkling wine,
But think of that so far off time.
The humble stable dark and bare
But filled with love so strong and fair.
That light will last for evermore,
So bright it lights up every shore.
But we must tend that wondrous flame,
Else none of us can shirk the blame
If that flame should go out.
So let's celebrate a day so fair
That each may have his rightful share
And faith may have no doubt.

B G Metcalfe

The Silent Past

They were like blind animals that burrow deep underground,
Breathing in the foul dust and gases that floats around,
They enter those box like cages into those blacken roads,
Where they sweat and toil digging those heavy loads.

They shine like glow-worms dancing at the dank pit head,
This is a unwelcoming place, the shadows the ghostly dead,
There are so many face peril and dangers in those tomb like places.
That blacken coal dust is so ingrained deeply upon their faces.

These miners who have died, this is their heartbreaking story,
This closed monument is now what's left of its former glory,
These brave men whose heads were held high and who walked tall,
They were husbands and sons killed by many rock falls.

Thro'out those long years the widows and children bear the pain
The ruling government we have closed the pits, what have they
                                                        gained?
They moved the slag heaps but the sorrow lies so long and deep
Where the lamp house stood only the ghosts now silently weeps.

You can tell an old miner as he struggles up a steep road.
Every agonising step you hear him coughing up his deadly load.
Where big wheel was is now silent you won't find its steel gates
To those dying colliers the coal dust have sealed their fate.

J F Grainger

The 20th Century

1900 the start of the new century there were wonders all around
This was the year that began the London Underground

The next few years cars arrived and man took to the air
Scott got to the South Pole to find Ammundsen had beaten him there

Titanic sank on her maiden voyage the pride of the White Star Line
Woolworth's started in New York, known as the nickel and dime

The 1914-18 War to end all wars, the worst that had ever been
Silent films were the rage, the Keystone Cops, things we'd never seen

Next came the roaring twenties and American Prohibition
The General Strike, the Charleston and the Great Paris Exhibition

Jolson spoke in the Jazz Singer saying, 'You Ain't Heard Nothing Yet!'
Mickey Mouse as Steamboat Willie a sure winner you can bet

The thirties brought depression in the states and also over here
The rise of the Nazi party, and Hitler was to become the biggest fear

The Spanish Civil War, persecution of the Jews, then peace in our time
The war that had to come, on Sept 3rd Nineteen Thirty-Nine.

The forties started with the Battle of Britain, the Blitz and Evacuees
In 1945 the Atom Bomb, what could have been worse than these

The fifties the Conquest of Everest, the Coronation, Rock and Roll
Then the Korean War broke out another that was to take it's toll

The sixties brought the Beatles, Kennedy's death, first man on the moon
Flower Power, which promoted peace, but this was to be over soon

In the seventies the Vietnam war, and streakers seen at Lords
Spaghetti Junction opened and a tennis triple win for Bjorn Borg

The eighties brought the Falklands war and many more disasters
Bradford stadium fire, the Heysel crush, then Hillsborough came after

The Gulf war in the Nineties then Croatia, Bosnia when will it ever end?
I pray that the year two thousand will have only peace to send

Dennis Stallard

The Butterfly

Oh, how I envy thee
Floating high above me
Flying through the gentle breeze
To come and go
As you please
Majestic wings, with colours so bold
Come to me, for I long to hold
Will you not settle
Upon my flowers of gold
Shimmering, shining
With grace and flair
Do not mind me, I only stare.

David John Smith

Someone You Know?

She sits alone -
Nowhere to go, no-one to see.
In the distance,
the sound of laughter penetrates her silence.
Happy, young and carefree,
friends together, with places to go.

Once again, the silence perpetrates her world
like a wanton dream.
The clock is chiming.
The silence, once again repeats the sadness of being alone.
Nowhere to go, no-one to see.
Perhaps tonight will be the one to end her dream.
Death, sweet death,
please come to me this evening,
that I may join my loved one gone before me.

The daylight comes,
Her warmth and light shine into the room.
The old lady opens her eyes
and marvels at the joy of hearing the dawn chorus of friendly chatter.
Spring is here - a new beginning.
She reflects on her thoughts from the evening before.
Loneliness is a terrible thing.
Perhaps today will be the day,
that someone will call?

Lisa A Hopkins

Resolutions

The bells will soon be ringing
To herald the new year,
And once again I must decide -
Resolution time is here.
Should I give up chocolate
And get a sylph-like figure,
Or maybe go and join a gym
To fill myself with vigour.
I've never had a lot of luck
With resolutions past,
Whatever I decided on
Just never seemed to last.
But in the year 2000
I promise I'll succeed
To kick the filthy habit
Of smoking that old weed.
I'm going to improve my life -
I know it's time well spent,
Even though the path to Hell
Is paved with good intent.

Angela George

If Your Love Was The Sun

If your love was the sun
I'd bathe in it all day
like a mad dog and an Englishman
I'd sun myself away

I'd languish in a pool of gold
you'd sink into my skin
fast flowing melted butter
where rays and beams set in

Then your love's sun will colour me
I'd have the darkest tan
deeper than Turkana
bigger than Sudan

Even in the ice age
your sun would still be here
to worship and fall into
making every blizzard clear

Hazel Houldey

The Natural World Around Us

I love the flowers:
I can while away the hours
Drinking in their charm,
Which to my troubled soul is balm.

I love the birds' song
Which echoes all day long:
To listen to their quavering trill
Is such an inexpressible thrill.

I love the humming of the bees
Buzzing among the flowers and trees:
Their honey has a delicious taste,
Far too precious to allow to waste.

I love the meandering streams;
I hear them sometimes in my dreams:
They make a gurgling sound
As they flow over the stony ground.

I love to see the distant hills,
Sometimes, sadly, quite close to grimy Mills;
But I know that wherever they stand,
Some beauty is always close at hand.

I love the tall and stately trees,
Their leaves fluttering in the breeze:
Some have survived unnumbered years,
The sight of them moving many a one to tears.

Last of all, I love the sky,
A reminder that the Creator of it all is nigh:
With Nature so full of beauty to the brim,
Surely we should bow down and worship Him.

Kenneth E Jinks

Mankind

Funny faces, mysterious places,
People moving, counting paces.
People angry, people sad,
People happy, people glad.

Many minds all wandering by,
Some quite low, others high;
Thinking of this complex world.
How their minds just twist and twirl!

Angry motions thwart their limbs,
Sometimes, a her sometimes a him,
Peoples' lives are so entwined.
Think of others, if you've the time.

Where is this love for all mankind?
Is it only in the mind?
We are just a selfish race
Keeping up with life's fast pace.

Time for others we have none,
Thinking just of our own fun.
Think of others for a change
Whatever colour, sex or age.

Jeanette Williams

He Will Come Again

Be prepared for we know not when
We'll see our maker face to face,
'Our Father who art in Heaven'
The day is coming, a miracle will have taken place.

Will our master walk upon the sea . . .
Stand beneath the rainbow
Come on a cloud for all to see
How will we know?

Will the mountains part, and the bride of Heaven appear
Will we fall on bended knee
Stand in wonder or in fear.
How many of us will be worthy?

Will all the evil darkness fade away
And the light sine brighter still,
Will that be our judgement day
The saving of souls - His will?

'He will come again' so it is said
The second coming of our Lord
With a golden crown upon his head
'Tis the truth, His word . . . Amen.

Deirdre Maria West

Shadows Of The Mind

Memories are the shadows of the mind,
Realities without substance
That life, in living, left behind,
Remembered proofs of your existence.

Memories are the you that used to be,
Stepping stones to take you back
To the life you used to have,
Before time moved you down the track.

Memories are the videos of the mind
With instant playback guaranteed,
Pre-historic high-tech recall,
And gaps with power to mislead.

Graham Jones

The Pen-y-Banc Brook Near Llandeilo

I walk by a Welsh brook
Which runs near Pen-y-Banc.
Water which hates stones
Like annoying children
Impeding its flowing movements
Gentling on towards the Towy.

Long, straggling and hair-like
Coarse grasses trail
Along sun-baked banks
Cracked and dry
From hot sun
Gentling on towards the Towy.

Large boulders loom ahead,
Menacing giants, long-unyielding,
But soon obstacles overcome
With centuries old perseverance
Of never-ending tumbling, skipping
Gentling on towards the Towy.

Wearily winding travelling on
Till motivated by storms hurrying.
Grass all soaking,
Banks a quagmire,
No longer children and giants hindering,
Rushing on towards the Towy.

Laura Föst

Islands

Islands so far away
Land of mist covered hill
Black faced sheep
Puffins seals and highland cattle
Viking ruins that tells of Ancient Battle
These are the memories to keep
Peat bogs and rugged cliff a land so still
A land that calls me and I must go
Back to those islands beyond the Scapa Flow
Home to that land so far away
Islands so stark so bare
My heart, my soul has always been there
Crofters and fisherfolk of yore
Ancestors heard whispering on the shore
Sense the magical atmosphere
As the harbour draws near
Now I am home at last
On those islands beyond the Scapa Flow

Hazel Smith

Pontyclûn - Mid Glam (Part Of The 20th Century)

The village was drowsy, a few cottages
Dotted here and there until the trains came.
So diminutive that the railway station was named
After the town on the hill that observed its life
As a grandfather does as he beguilingly watches
His grandchildren at play. Days rolled on in a
Halcyon manner, the arrival of a child, the departure
Of a villager was the stimulating news -
The war was happening in some far off place

A few men were leaving, ration books were important.
But food was quite adequate, air raids were rare
Then all changed; it was nineteen forty-three
The transformation began: Sir Rees no longer lived in the Manor
House
Soldiers on crutches in vivid blue uniforms with
Ties of scarlet that splashed like blood against their white shirts
Convalesced in the ancient splendour
Llanelay Hall housed the Bakery Corps - crusty
Loaves for hungry troops everywhere.

The doorways housed small dark men
Gambling with dominoes their crumpled brown
Uniforms and caps denoting they were a long way from Italian shores
Open lorries passed through with barbed wire sides
Blonde troops guarded by an armed Sergeant -
Rushing to work in the fields.
American GIs gave their gum to the children and girls
Tired lined and lank Polish refugees worked the iron-ore mines
And lovely women's skin turned yellow from work in the munitions
Factories.

All had changed - the war had arrived at Pontyclûn
Memories of childhood, a long time ago, fear and
Excitement a new world to know: lessons to be
Learnt, emotions to feel, years of jubilation
Of sadness to sow.

Joan Richardson

Looking Forward

The Country feels, with Domes and Wheels,
It can commemorate
The passing of two thousand years
On one momentous date.

But how will these fine landmarks
Withstand the test of time?
Will they stop wars and poverty?
Curb anarchy and crime?

Or should we help the people -
The coming generation?
They are the ones who'll influence
The outlook of our nation.

They'll make the rules or break the rules
And change the face of home.
So should we spend on our future
Or exhibits in The Dome?

Susan M Wilson

Believe In The Beast

Bemused, beguiled, bedraggled in bedlam,
beyond battlements blackened by bitumen,
between brandished broadswords battles are born,
the blood bathers breast stroke begins.
Baal bellowed at the brutes from above,
'Begone brave boys, blessed be the bountiful,
bestill the belligerence,' he blazed.
But Beelzebub arose behind the bosses back,
blackening the brightness with black magic abound.
'I bestow a beast on you bedevilled brothers,
behold the Basilisk, biting far worse than its bark.'
The behemoth with blazing breath belched,
over the bewildered blood-letters with bile.
Bodies burned, their bellicose souls beseeching,
and were brought before the blackest bishop begging.
Branded and beaten, bones broken beyond time,
the basest being adds baubles to its bracelet.
Beware the 'bette noire' biding time,
laying bets the barbarians blow bad once more,
bringing out the beast from beneath Scotia's brooding Ness.

Martin Richmond

Goodbye

Now that it's time to say goodbye,
    My heart is full of sadness;
The sun has gone beyond the sky,
    Taking with it all my gladness:
The dignified splendour has gone from the tree,
    The colour has gone from the flower;
No star of hope shineth for me,
    To lighten this darkened hour.

As I lie here alone with my solitary grief,
    Adreading the oncoming day;
Seeking in vain for some comforting relief,
    From this constant misery:
I know that in my heart you will always dwell,
    Even until the day I die;
So I pray this may only be a temporary farewell,
    And not a final goodbye.

John Kelly

Shetland Summer

Here, on this summer cliff top, there's a kingdom at my feet,
With lichened stones and ancient rocks where timeless breakers beat,
A windy world of winging joy, of breathless soaring flight,
The airy maze of circling tern, the gannet's dizzying height.

Here, on this summer cliff top, there's a kingdom in my hands;
A forest of small moss cups with bejewelled spider strands.
There's tangy thyme and clover, a silver nacre shell,
A pebble worn so smooth by years, so old that none can tell.

Here, on this summer cliff top, there's kingdom in my soul,
A sense of space, eternity, high, limitless, yet whole,
Defined and yet unbounded, and light as morning's wings,
Brief summer's life, Mortality, Change and unchanging things.

Stella Shepherd

Ecstasy

I stood on the threshold, waiting, expecting to here His voice,
My body tense, tuned in to the least rustle
From branches and leaves tossing overhead.

Then came a breeze, light as a cobweb limned in morning sun -
Yet this was not His voice -
Was it, then, a harbinger, like distant bell?

My heart's longing called out its hunger -
To here one word that would bid me come, and
    enter His sacred Presence.

Memories from other times stirred like autumn leaves
Wine-coloured in maturity from touch of burning sun.

Where are you then, my Beloved one?
I wait in lonely longing, for I love you so -

No sound, no word between us, but suddenly
His arms enfold me in close embrace -
One with my Beloved - my ecstasy complete.

    Kay Rowley

Glances

T S Eliot my mind in a spin
to read to learn thinking of him
Put pen to paper a clever man
I guess it's easy when you can

Shelley, Byron side by side
Poe and Kipling, they can't hide
The poets surely everlasting
inspire my thoughts in even starting

Declare to say the world goes on
with good fellows such, who contribute so much
To love to life in every way
giving joy in each day

Death has illumined the land of sleep
Longfellow said it, that was sweet
Literally world don't go away
a poem will always make my day . . .

Jean Tennent Mitchell

Saga Of Two Scottish Cities

Edinburgh city is mighty pretty with
Its castle, palace and St Gile's cathedral too.
But to class it with 'No mean city' Glasgow really will not do!
Glasgow's ship building record was second to none!!
And Edinburgh's festival is both for education and fun!!
'Glaswegian' humour can be earth 'tis true
Bu the kindness of the 'citizens'
Has helped unknown people from Scotland to Peru!!
While the 'Edinburghites' considered by some to be 'uppish and cool'
When it comes to 'homelessness' or 'children in need'
They excel in great humanity yes indeed!!
So while 'the cities' may be culturally and commercially apart
They are forever linked together by 'their peoples'
Large and ever loving 'Scottish hearts'!!
Especially in this 'the millennium year'
When with a 'parliament' of our own and 'national unity'
We as a 'proud and ancient people' can help to educate the world
Without favour or fear!!

Flora Divers

The Setting Sun

Some nights we see when day is done
The glorious setting of the sun.
Dark clouds outlined with gold
So wondrous to behold.

Pale blue and a ridge of darkest grey
Running full length on the Horizon.
Purple tints, then a snow white cloud
Like a lamp lit behind a shroud.

With deepest sighs
I fix my eyes.
This glory bright
Is a wonderful sight.

Now a blend of pink and grey
I cannot pull my gaze away.
No earthly artist can compete
With God's creations so complete.

Dorothy Hill Bradshaw

Her Life
(In memory of my late mother Dorothy Patricia Webb (Bartlett))

Born the youngest child of five,
In a one bedroom flat they have to survive.
Their mother works both night and day,
Just for a small pittance of pay.
A bottom drawer is used for her cot,
For money there was never a lot.
Their father worked, sometimes not legal,
He got caught by the Justice Of Eagle.
Leaving their mother all alone,
Working and fighting for a larger home.
Their father quietly played away,
Leaving his wife and children to pay.
Another woman the father went to live,
Their mother she could never forgive.
Working and struggling for a better life,
Their mother now just simply an ex wife.
He asked for forgiveness and to come back,
But like in work not to be trusted he was given the sack.
At the age of fourteen her father passed away,
Not really knowing him, no words to say.
Years went by she seen her mother's pain,
Would she never have a life again?
She never seen complete happiness in her mother's face,
All her mother's heartache left her at her final resting place.
Without all the heartache trouble and pain,
She sometimes wonders in heaven if they are together again.

Sylvia Mudford

Hometown Girl

She's a valley's girl I heard the shout
Casting a glance to the corner
Where the lads hang out
As walking towards them
Fixed expressions to see
Their cold staring eyes
Sent a chill running through me

Pausing for a minute, composure to regain
Feet ready to take flight
Heart pounding wildly inside
Taking a deep breath and with a turn of the head
I continued on my way

Light spots of rain had started falling
As journeying on through my old hometown
Reviving memories best forgotten
But eager to see the old place again

The sound of a clock chiming in the distance
A landmark that still remained
Of an industrial era in our history
And part of our heritage so it became

Looking round at the changes where old
Then new now stand side by side
Gone was the character of those buildings
That had stood the test of time
A new shopping precinct had been born within
Leaving behind
The quaintness and simplicity from years gone by.

Valerie Thompson

The Seasons

Spring came dancing over the earth,
And lambs came out to play.
I thought about the Lamb of God
Who gave his life away.

Then summer strolled across the scene,
And I walked by the sea.
I thought about the one, who calmed
The waves, on Galilee.

Soon, autumn dashed upon the stage
With colours bright and bold.
I thought about a king, whose crown
Was thorns, instead of Gold!

Winter crept in with silent snow,
And day was dark as night.
I thought about God's only Son
Who came to bring us light.

For all the people in this world
Wherever they may be
In changing seasons, He is here,
His love is clear to see.

Audrey Parks

magic

convents closed,
deserted the cathedrals
since the king has coupled
monks and nuns
and sent them on their way
in quest of
skin beneath their cowls.

gone the magic of the chants and incense
rising to the beams along the roof.
'assumpta est in caelum
virgo, dei genetrix',
they used to sing convincingly, convinced,
'a virgin beamed to heaven
as her womb was used by god'.

belief in miracles
endured the centuries
until one realised
that footprints in the sand,
if feet indeed did touch the ground,
were blown away by wind and rain
millennia ago.

magic is a christmas tree with candlelight,
a fire full of flaming wood, ajar a window
as an invitation to the christ-child
not to pass us by, but leave some presents
you, of course, have paid for, even
wrapped in red striped paper, but remember:
magic is the magic of belief and make believe.

Fred W Kroese

Fallen Leaves

Outside my window it was snowing leaves.
Red, orange, yellow and brown they descended,
Covering the pavements with a crisp meringue coating.
Childlike, I delighted in the crackling sound
As I crunched them beneath my feet.
In a short few weeks only a solitary leaf hung on,
Grimly clinging to black skeletal branches
That outlined the grey and misty skyline.
An autumn downpour soon reduced
The gleeful fluttering leaves to a sodden mass,
Clogging the drains and blocking the downpipes.
I cursed them loudly as I crouched in the pouring rain
Clearing them away.

P H Thomas

Misunderstood

How beautiful she was
With rain crystals in her hair, yet
Beauty is not enough
to satisfy this bitter world.

Today I am followed
how still I am now; with these my
Memories drifting down
the sun has not forgotten me.

Sleep with your spirit; and
Let your heart, with its edges, scream
I am lost, but my dreams
are solid and frozen by time.

It is best to hide now
Sleep will never calm my dazed mind
What I can remember
is barely realised, somehow.

    Strawberry Fields-Forever

Stonehenge

On Salisbury Plain, the ring of stones stands for all to see
And anyone who passes by, wonders how it came to be.
Who were the ancient builders who set the circle there?
Was it an observatory or a place of prayer?
Did they worship the sunrise of a solstice dawn
Or was it the lights creator that they called upon?
The druids in their robes of white would worship there today.
If travellers fighting with police did not keep them away.
That's not the reason it was built, not how it should be.
The builders who created it worked in unity.
They must have worked together, or that ring could not be built.
Those who would destroy its peace should be filled with guilt.
To all who wish to visit there, whatever your Gods my be.
Honour those ancient builders. Go in peace and harmony.

Pamela Evans

Endless

Waves rip and ride over the reflective surface,
Setting the sea alight with the endless cycle of water,
Moving to crash the beaten shore,
Shafts of light shine down from the clouded sky,
Birds span gliding for eternity on a journey with no end.

Wind, whips the sand into frenzy,
As it dances across the ever-shifting plains,
Distant figures walk the sand,
Forgotten, before ever being remembered,
Casting empty shadows over,
The water in silent hope.

Jessica Johnson

The Welsh

The dragon lives on peaks and in valleys
The scarlet demon in the hearts of men
The heat of his fire has tempered their souls
The roar of a nation for the men in his colours
Supporting them onwards as the tests arise
With passion and for glory we take on the world
From near and far they come to take up the challenge
To see who's the strongest the quickest the best
So assemble the colours of every nation
All in one place our nation's own capital
To play and do battle on our hallowed turf
To raise the world cup in the millennium stadium
So with hope and with pride we raise our sweet voices
To lift up the spirits and urge them do well
We sing out together the sweet songs of Wales.

Kelvin Kriescher

Are You Coming Out To Play?

Silently I stood there,
In the midst of nothing more.
As clouds sped by overhead,
The same as years before.

Now there were no friendly faces,
No laughter or good cheer.
They had disappeared with the time,
I was alone now standing here.

There is grass now growing beneath my feet,
Where the cobble stones used to be.
The creamstone and the sandstone steps,
I can no longer see.

The ragbone man has also gone,
Disappeared into a rainy afternoon.
But he had always made it bright for me,
With a stick and a little balloon.

This is where street lamp halo's shone,
Flickering in the night.
As childish minds sat and watched,
The dancing shadows of warming light.

Now there is only daylight,
For like the clouds they have flown away.
I shall never hear those words again,
'Are you coming out to play?'

R V Denton

Remember Aberfan's Sorrow 1966

'Wales' The land of song, and sorrows,
For today, and all tomorrows,
A huge cross for all to see,
A generation of children, 'Dear God', suffer them to come to thee,
Deep in the pits, men sweat, and toil;
Breathing gasps, as lungs are rasped, and lives spent, as beneath a fall
of coal, there's turmoil,
As men are crushed, to dig no more, the price of coal, no more to
pay;
But, God in Heaven, as we kneel here to pray,
Knew not we, that our little ones, we would lose this day,
For all our work and toil;
The muck, we threw out, on thy soil;
Did watch it grow, so black and menacing, yet on we went, till too
late,
Did watch it pass over a school, and its gate,
With screams, and cries, that we will remember,
Smothered for ever;
Oh! 'Dear God' their pain, their fears,
Our little generation, has left us in tears,
The land of song, has borne its cross,
And we mourn, Our Great Loss!

Irene Beynon

Hearts Content

I think of you and know
you think of me sometimes
images floating as a cloud
on giddy heights

Don't meet often when we do
rest of the world goes by
you saw my need
of a friend, in deed
steadfast and true

Like the air we breath
seen giving light
attuned again
to universe

Mary Hughes

A Whispering Wind

A whispering wind spoke to me.
Within its vision I could see
Fields of green brooks and glens
In this changing world which God defends.

Buildings of stone keep us warm
When thunderous clouds bring such storms
Love and hope remain the same
As we play this ageing game.

Winter summer all year long
Little songbirds sing their song.
High upon a mountain's top
Music makes this planet rock.

Concrete roads shooting stars
Is there really life on Mars.
Air we breathe life depends
On this changing world which God defends.

Cities fuelled with numerous powers
Time is measured by the hours
Death or drugs increasing stakes
For every soul a dealer takes

Joy that fills enchanted places
Babies born with tiny faces.
Each passing day I often smile
Listen to the wind a while.

Just like the moon and setting sun
All of us are blessed as one.
This is where my vision ends
In this changing world which God defends.

R Connor

The Wily Fox

Oh wily one, what have you done?
For poor ole fox is on the run.
Out of the wilderness, she took her chance
And led the hounds, a merry dance.
Over undergrowth, marshes and rocks
Losing her scent - that's got them foxed.
She didn't realise, she was in the race
And led them on a wild goose chase.
Wading through dunes, and bogs
While it rained cats and dogs
Panting mutts, shake off the wet.
For they haven't caught old Foxy yet
For she'll go, around another lap
For she won't fall, into their trap.
The hunt is on, the bugle blown
The horses dressed, the grouse have flown
For just her snout, visible to see
In the cover of an old oak tree
Her ears prick up at barking sound.
She cowers frightened, in the ground.
They've lost her scent, thanks to the rain
She's got away, with her life again.
This time the fox they didn't slay
For she lives to fight another day.

C Mogford

Dolphins And Whales

I hear on tape beneath the sea
Of dolphins, whales. Of souls they be.
A magic grace, a water's tide
Embrace their charm, sweet liquid pride.

I hear in home beneath the sea
A gift, a world, an ink to me.
As babies scream in search of word,
So dolphins play. Life's not absurd.

I hear in awe beneath the sea
Of whales profound in giantry.
The foolish vowels greed and men
Impose on God sweet time again.

I hear in salt beneath the sea
A beauty to transfigure free
All who hurt and fear in vain
The deathing shadow of life's gain.

I hear, I feel beneath the sea
The anguished hurt whose skin is thee.
O do not be afraid, dear friend.
For God is good and love, the end.

Hywel Davies

I Can't Forget

A cup of tea
A last cigarette
Then off to bed to try and forget
Fire out bottle filled
All ready?
Not I feel a trifle heady
Switch out light
Pull back sheet
I hope tonight my dreams are sweet
Put myself right
Tuck myself in
Must try now not to think of him
Thoughts of work
Or counting money
My - but his lips did taste of honey
Stop it now
Try and guide your mind
Oh but he was really kind
What to wear
Which skirt? Which top?
Thoughts are wandering I must stop
Go to sleep
If only I can
All I need is my man
I can't forget
It's hard to do
I thought his love for me was true

Beryl Spanswick

Perfect Peace

I know a wood
Where scented violets grow
Where bluebells under trees
Soft breezes blow
And there the snake
Lies basking in the sun
And tiny rabbits from their burrows run
Far up above are squirrels
In the trees
They leap from branch to branch
With greatest ease
As daylight fades and shadows fall
The nightingale and forest owls do call
This is a place where only you can find
Peace with the world
And perfect peace of mind.

    Sylvia Bryan

Alone, Again

Soft and swiftly, sweeps the darkness,
wrapping me in deepest night.
It holds me safe until the daybreak,
reminds me that you're far away.

Hands that held the lovely flowers
stoop to pick their petals up,
from the table where we placed them,
before you went so far away.

I fancy that I hear your voice,
even your foot upon the stair.
The mind can play such teasing tricks,
I know too well, you're far away.

Such traces of you soon will fade,
as though you were not here at all,
but not the tender love you showed me,
or your paintings on my wall.

Megan Guest

Another Aberystwyth Sunday

Rock music comes from the football club
Aberystwyth are playing a foreign team
Traffic is bad as usual on Penglais Hill
The sun is out, people are on the move
Children are on the swings in the park
Wimbledon hopefuls play tennis on the courts
In the cemetery there is perfect peace
Just a breeze to ruffle the trees
From the station the steam train hoots
Ready to depart for a trip to Devil's Bridge
Just another Aberystwyth Sunday.

Melanie M Burgess

The Mind

A befuddled mind, fighting the mist,
As past becomes the present,
Incapable of defining which
It truly is unpleasant.

They say it is Alzheimer!
She never will get better.
Terror and fear are her intimate friends,
Never knowing any other.

There are times when she is lucid,
As sane as you or I.
Yet can turn with a vengeance
In the blink of an eye.

You love this woman who gave you life,
After all, she is your mother.
Her ranting and raving tears you apart,
You desperately wish it was another.

Though tonight you said she knew you.
Her eyes showed she remembered your birth.
With trickling tears, she held your hand tight
As she sadly left this earth.

In the Lord's hands she now is cradled,
Her memory true and bright.
You too may get Alzheimer.
Pray God: you never forget this night.

Denise Winstone

The Last Attack

With thunderous roar the marching Zulus came
Along the skyline of the Shiyane Hill.
Blood lust was in their veins - the urge to kill,
To dispossess the British of their claim.

Their spears flashed like lasers in the sun,
And through the haze with cool precision sped.
Then scarlet tunics turned to deeper red;
The final, savage onslaught had begun.

Like stormy billows crashing on the shore,
For weary hours they swamped the barricades.
At last they dropped their shields to fight no more
Against the bayonets and fusillades.
They praised their foes, then left the valley floor
To vanish in the early morning shades.

This sonnet was written from the Zulus' point of view.

Celia G Thomas

2000, What's Changed?

A clean page, a new year,
who knows what will be.
I only know when the fuss
dies down, I will still be me.

Age will paint my face
showing the mark of time,
I'll fight the flab, tell off
the kids, enjoy a glass of wine.

Get of out bed, go off to work,
enjoying my daily bread.
Hoping that life's expectations
don't go over my head.

My life has been very busy,
it's had its ups and downs,
I've had many a moment of jollity
and endured some horrible clowns.

Having said all that I'm still smiling,
mostly in good cheer, so here to
all my friends and foes alike
'I wish you all a great new year!'

May Lewis

Magical Lovers
(Dedicated to Tereza Balakova of the Czech Republic)

We ride white horses
Through fantasy land
A fairytale romance
Embraced in passionate dance.

We ride white horses
Through magical times
A prince and princess
Lost in their poems and rhymes.

We ride white horses
Through eternity
Enchanted lovers in ecstasy
Look to the stars
Can you see 'magic white horses'
Onward to destiny.

Peter John

Steam-v-Diesel

Taking a train journey just isn't the same
Now that most trains do not run on steam.
When I think of trips that I made
When quite young, it is as though it
Was all just a dream.

The diesels go faster and are more clean.
Yet they don't really give the same thrill
As the beautiful steam machine.

It is just as well most children these days
Do not know what they are missing,
Or else, back to the good old days of
Steam is what they would be wishing.

Though the diesel is much better you know
They will never convince me that this is indeed so.

Anna Aldridge

The Last Rebels Of Change

Quiet, Peace and Sanity,
These are the victims of change.
Stress, Rush and Calamity,
Are all in touching range.
Some refuse the bait of Progress:
Easy life, shorter work.
They would rather recess,
To the fruits of times Past.
Quiet Peace and Sanity,
These are the victims of change.
When worded like this,
It does sound strange,

Find some time,
Before it Runs out.

Chris McParland (12)

Rain

This world we inhabit is a wonderful place.
If we listen and look and slow down a pace.
The beauty is evident, the mystery sublime
The wonders of nature, and all this is mine
Yours too, each one of us must hold on to this treasure
It must be nurtured and kept for ever
We are responsible, we hold the key
It must be respected, by you and by me.
The givers of life are around us each day
Each one respected and loved in its way.
But one that returns, again and again
Without it we'd die life giver - the rain.

It starts with a patter, a plop and a splash.
The raindrops get bigger and thunder may crash
The flowers and plants, the birds and the trees
Open their petals, their wings and their leaves
To catch all the moisture that falls from the sky
This giver of life on which we rely
It forms into puddles and gathers in pools
When caught in the sunlight, it sparkles like jewels.
Once started, the raindrops get busier now
Birds huddle together, wet through on the bough
Rivulets run excitedly by
Till the rivers are reached and then with a sigh
They join the mad rush of waters so deep
Get stronger and swifter as onward they leap
The earth drinks its fill, replenished at last
The overflow, joining their river so fast
And so life evolves the rivers in flood
Flows over its bank and stratifies mud
The sun plays a role and returns to the scene
Transforming the water into vapour and steam
Up in the atmosphere, there to remain
Until nature returns it to earth as the rain.

Heather Aguis

Missing

I remember when dreams seemed obtainable
A time when my world had no boundaries
The future was too bright to see
When did the illusion shatter

Disappointment becoming all too familiar
I became the creator of my own limitations
Now I sit alone cynical and jaded
Waiting for the sun to shine again

Unable to relax in fear of what may be around the corner
Terrified to hope for anything more than survival
The success of other's reminding me of my failures

So here I stay trying to sift through the landscape of my mind
In search of something that is missing
Unsure if I ever possessed it in the first place
Perhaps it was an illusion, a cruel dream to make life harder

Perhaps it has never left
It has been right here in front of me all the time
And I have been too blind to see
Dwelling in darkness, unable to notice and embrace the light

Glyn Mann

The Reluctant Patriot

This is a land whose heights
Are storm-washed in perpetuity
Tossed cliff-shales pebbled
By land-greedy tides.

With needle-sharp shores that
Kidnap into flotsam
A vessel insouciant
Complacent, malwatched.

Yet here in high solstice
Safe younglings may delve
Surprising a castle
Ready-sculped 'neath her sands.

She may ennoble at times
One common man as hero
Beyond the imagination of the proletariat
Who million-perish unremarked.

For all her caprices undefendable
In her kinder she may yet
Inspire a devotion and even
Unto sacrifice an affection.

Because it happened to one of mine,
I know this to be true.

    Sarah Blackmore

A Rainbow Of Thoughts

When after a mighty downpour,
    the sun comes out with a smile.
There is often a magical rainbow,
    that is spanning many a mile.

Perhaps it begins in a river
    then slips into a puddle of rain.
But the glorious rainbow of colours,
    in my heart will always remain.

There's the red of a glorious sunset
    to the end of a perfect day.
The orange of glowing embers,
    fireside warmth begs me to stay.

Yellow daffodils, buttercups, cowslips.
    Just how did it all begin?
The green of the grassy mountains,
    hiding the valleys within.

The blue of the sky in its glory,
    that enhances the hue of the sea.
But where indigo comes from, I know not.
    It just seems all purple to me!

At the end of the spectrum -
    sweet violet.
Be it flower or a marvellous hue.
    It's aura dances around me.
And I start to see things anew.

    Cherry Eccles

Wedding Day

As your wedding day dawns upon this morn
May all God's blessings upon you adorn.
As you stand together side by side
Saying your vows with love and pride
Only tears of joy you will shed
When you think of the years of happiness which lie ahead.
Now man and wife you are as one
Your life together has just begun.
Caring and sharing in sickness and in health
Love in abundance is the meaning of wealth.

Gwyneth E Scott

If I Could

There is so much injustice in the world,
Whatever happened to the good?
So much cheating, lying, stealing
                        people's lives,
I'd put it all right if I could.

There is so much pain felt by everyone,
Whatever happened to the love?
So much hurt and crying, dying
                        of the souls,
I'd try to heal it if I could.

There is so much darkness in all our lives,
Whatever happened to the light?
Where is the laughing, smiling, glowing
                        from within?
I'd give it all back if I could.

    Kim Fry

My Mother's Day

I bring no flowers to you this Mother's Day:
Your grave lies far from here and out of reach;
But in my heart, much lovelier than any short-lived blooms
My love for you endures and blossoms bright.

These flowers I keep for you, across long years
Await the day, *my* Mother's Day,
When, with my love, I put them in your hands
And, for Eternity, try gladly to repay
The dear, unstinting care your love bore me.

A C Dunsmore

The Dual City Of Swansea

Long known for its duality,
The twin named town
Where worlds collide
Sits cradled in the crescent;
Smoke pervades ev'ry crook and nanny,
Ev'ry street and dimlight alley,
And people toil up longer hills
Earning less and more reward.
A Gower gate it stands surprised,
Growth unchecked and pastures green,
Present a journey to those who gaze,
Four walls reflect the mind that glares.
Miniature cultures hide divides,
Young and old jostle side by side,
Scorching or freezing, facing the sun,
A magnet city with a toe in the ocean.

Andrew Smith

Cold Mornings

The sky paints the winter
Dawning curls.
Life is something different,
And the words that I said didn't say what I meant.
You are my all and my reason,
You are every fall and every truth and timeless treason,
Always there, within, without, and part of me,
My chagrin, my doubt, you shadow the cores of me.

I don't need to see you,
To stay your walk,
To make you stop and smile and talk,
Or take you to me.
There is no why or where,
Just the secret and the silence that you are out here,
And in there.

The days are like snowflakes,
You walk flowers,
Tread question marks through the mist,
Forever shines and freezes,
But it's a beautiful never ever,
And never to be kissed.

Laura Smith

Cardiff Bay

Like twisted sculptures on a mirrored glass, they stand,
Once proud reminders of a vanished past
When ships would come
From distant shore, to trade in coal
And grain and ore
At Cardiff Dock

No vessels now will ever moor
At these stark piles
Nor children tread the boards, long gone,
With eager fare, for Bristol
Or for Weston-Super-Mare

The mirror shatters as the ebb tide flows
Exposing to the glistening sun
A thousand facets of the mud-caked shore.
I shade my eyes against the glare
But dancing yet, upon the retina of memory I see
Their silhouette

The ebb tide goes from Cardiff Bay
And as the final curtain falls
Who then recalls its ebbs and flows?
And is it for the best,
Who knows?
But doubtless I'll be there
Applauding man's strange opera
With all the rest

Tim Raikes

Hope

Darkness falls, how cold the night,
Soon to be lilt by pale moonlight.
A fox will steal from its lair
While the shriek from an owl will raise your hair.

A little hedgehog will snuffle around
Keeping its nose down to the ground.
A little mouse from its home will creep
Hope against hope that the cat will sleep.

Not all will sleep the hours away,
Night will be just as busy as day.
The sick to be tended,
Bones to be mended.

A good fight fought may well be lost
Or may be won at whatever the cost.
The tears will fall as a soul departs
Leaving behind broken hearts.

But even though a life will sever,
Darkness does not last forever.
And as the shadows of the night,
Fade into dawn's early light,

The cry of a babe newly born
Will enter into a bright new morn.
Though loved ones lost will remain in your heart,
For in your life they have played a part.

From the tunnel of darkness you will venture,
And a warm sunny day you will enter.
Sad memories will fade away,
But joyous ones will always stay.

J Mary Dobbinson

Houses

Houses small, houses large,
To buy a nice one, what's the charge,
Houses, houses all around,
Some with pretty gardens bound.

Some are long, some are tall,
Surrounded by a garden wall,
Some are brick, some are stone,
Every one is someone's home.

Mansions, bungalows and flats,
Space for people and their cats,
Homes with windows of all sizes,
A place of refuge in a crisis.

Houses red, houses white,
Be it wrong or be it right,
Filled with furniture and with beds,
The perfect place to lay our heads.

Some have budgies, some have dogs,
Garden ponds all filled with frogs,
Some have patios, some have lawns,
Sparkling gems when morning dawns.

Houses, houses everywhere,
Standing up to weather's wear,
Without our houses where would we be,
Probably living rough in cardboard citee!

Aileen Mathieson

Dignity

I know people say 'well it's okay for them
just lay in their bed and send off their claim'
Or call at the centre now there is a laugh
rejection again by such uncaring staff.
A labourer's job - now for that I would strive
what's that you said, don't bother, I am over twenty-five?
I wonder what they're thinking as they yet again dismiss me,
do they ever stop, think, look beyond the statistics - see me.
See the feeling of helplessness, hurt, anger, despair,
behind this faceless person, cast aside without a care.
The hopes, the dreams of days gone by, set aside to who knows when
until the time I get a job, and I can feel in control again
For now I face the world alone with no self-esteem at all
getting by from day to day, my back against the wall.
So look you people who are safe - secure, I used to be like you
and think but for the grace of God you could feel like this too.
So look with eyes, mind, heart, wide open - See
Then I can keep the one thing I still have
I'll keep my dignity.

B Symons

Silent Little Children Sleep

Silent little angels sleep
while parents, friends and hearts
must weep. The storm will pass
when wounds no longer bleed
and life wraps chains around
the brittle seed.

As time goes by, red turns to rust
and life goes on, because it must,
the place where hope and future died
is now a place where colour thrives.

L M Scott

Professionalism

The Royal British Legion Scotland Beating Retreat
held on the Edinburgh Castle Esplanade,
waiting for everybody to take their seat.

Across the Greatest draw bridge soon,
march and counter march, to those great tunes.
Pipers, drummers, fifty Standard bearers as well,
lone piper on the rampart high,
each and everyone looking swell.

Standards to the lower on the second or third *boom*.
Eight thousand seats, north, south and east
echoing in the greatest *toon*,
nothing to beat this spectacular retreat.

T H P Anderson

Sanctum

This summer place this precious land
More beauty than my eyes and ears can understand,
Shades of green and countless flowers
Sparkling lochs and leafy bowers.
This summer place where song birds sing
Filling the air and blessing everything,
There I find peace, from sadness I retire
And in some way I find my heart's desire.

Hannah Hepburn

Waterfoot In The Shadow - New Year

The wind whipped the waves,
Helping, not holding their advance
On the winter-water shoreline,
As creeping crustily, they cracked their record.

And rain rallied the watery hymn,
Made bold and blustering
By the whining wind;
Each drop defying its dread of death.

And care was abandoned to God
As the two-way-water soaked, pervaded,
And washed away earth unsecured by growth,
Leaving riverbank rubble uncovered again.

But with eyes of trust and hope,
I could see the copious provision
Of the watery robber's bounteous gifts,
Left behind for the time when seeds can grow.

And so, like Waterfoot in the New Year,
I rest content, unafraid of winter's ravages,
Trusting in the promises of God,
And the hope of Spring's rebuilding.

Heulwen Carrier

The Millennium

The new Century is approaching fast,
We hope for better things,
Like nicer people who care at last,
Who knows what the future brings,

Little children loved by all
Their parents need to care,
No drugs or killings should befall,
A safe world for all to share.

Let all evil be known in the past,
And be kind to one another,
Our Lord above will come at last,
To be with His sister and brother.

Is it only a dream or will it come true,
That we will all live in peace.
The sun will shine out of a sky of blue,
The dark clouds disappear and the evil will cease
So we will look forward to the new year,
With a joyous heart,
No more bad threats will we hear,
No more loved ones will part.

Elizabeth Greig

It Was Only The Beginning

On the tree that day
A man was crucified;
He hung in silent agony
For every eye to see,
They saw His nakedness and shame,
His suffering and pain,
They watched Him as He died.

Oppressed and afflicted He came,
Like a lamb He was slain;
Yet He bore it all for us -
The bruising of the Cross;
He drank the bitter cup because
He loved us, you and me,
Christ paid our debt on Calvary.

But that was not the end,
Christ loosed the power of Satan's hand
And with victory shout He rose again,
Death's keys were in His hand;
No longer on His head a crown of thorns
But upon His Kingly brow,
The Crown of Glory now adorns.

The cross may be empty now
It's work of redemption done,
But the effects of Christ's mission
       Continue on;
For His Spirit is ever near,
He's alive and lives in everyone
Who believe and follow Him.

    Ann Anderson

Untitled

I'm just a short distance from bliss.
I get closer each time we kiss.
The touch of your skin is exciting
And your open arms are inviting.
I want to be with you every night.
I want to see you by dawn's first light.
And when I watch you as you sleep
I know my feelings for you run deep.

Lorraine Swan

Dark Skies

Watching the news, unfold in front of my eyes
    I have to ask the insane reason why?
    Callous killing with fields so dry
    Chemical rain with a coloured dye
The inspired prophet holding up the sky
A distant star watched by NASAs roving eye.
    The first question raised
    Is the first person so bold?
    Tears for the war dead
    Remembered so cold.
The chemical waste fills the blood spewed heavens
The clouds transformed into a glowing remembrance
    A lost child, meets generation X
    A final reminder why I need a fix
    To sell this question, to relay my mind.
    Just numbing my thoughts from the
        Human mankind.

Richard C Scott

Trapped In The System

I sat in the midst of these professionals,
Psychiatrist, Psychologist and Occupational Therapist.
In my peripheral vision I could see my parental guardian,
Mouth open as if to speak, lips moved as they would,
No words came out, then I knew, the inner sanctum were in charge.
Their voices seemed so far away, how can that be?
When they're so near?

They talk as if I wasn't here,
The one in charge moves purposely to my side, hand on my shoulder
. . .
. . . Schizophrenic . . . do we all agree,
Poor soul, lost touch with reality.
Let's try medication x y zee.

They fed me with hallucinogenic drugs.
Then get angry when I won't bathe.
I tell them there's spiders in the bath,
But they just sneer at me.
A supervised bath, how degrading.
I protest, to no avail, you see I have no rights.
A section order seen to that.

It's five years on and I'm still here,
A shadow of what I used to be.
Swollen body, involuntary movement of my limbs,
Blurred vision, deafness in my ears,
No one ever sees my tears.
I caught a glimpse of someone in a mirror rocking to and fro,
They looked a lot like me,
No it can't be.

Mary Smith

So Like a Dream

Lying on a water-lily leaf -
    Relief he did not then make for the soil
        Filling me with fascination, awe -
    I saw him curled, relaxed, in speckled coil,
    Reflecting sun, as oil
Reflects its beams but rarely and as brief.

The gentle movement of the spring-fed stream
    Seemed to rock him into deeper sleep.
        I took my camera out. I meant to capture
    Rapture of a sleep so calm and deep,
    And vowed, that day, I'd keep
A record of a sight so like a dream.

My footsteps on the bridge I thought would wake
    And make him slither to a dark recess
        By swimming, sinuous, under water's cover;
    A lover of the dark, he'd soon progress,
    Away from fear and stress,
To a couch so much more suited to a snake.

But motionless he lay. In disbelief -
    Relief as well; I thought I'd seen death's sign -
        I watched. His skin with colours seemed to glow.
    No snake, I realised, dead, could be so fine,
    And with such grace recline,
Lying on a water-lily leaf.

Mabel Helen Underwood

The Future

Please don't feel embarrassed
Or inclined to turn away
I slept in this doorway yesterday -
I shall, again, today.

Not a sumptuous lifestyle
One I never chose
Circumstances - forced it,
They easily arose!

Therefore, don't be disgusted
Or have too critical a view
Be aware the unexpected -
May one day, befall you, too!!

Jean McVicar

The Cat

Cats are graceful
Cats are cool
Cats are so refined
A more hoi-poloiti animal
Would be hard to find.
You call them -
They ignore you,
'Can't you see I'm
Trying to nap'
And then before you know it
They are curled up
On your lap.
They suit themselves you see
The World is their domain
And that suits me just fine too
Because a world without the cat
Would never be the same.

Maureen Stuart

Committed

My commitment to you, is for eternity.
The love that's held, is meant to be.
United we'll be, in this coming year,
A plain, *'simple'* band, showing our unity.

People will know. Some witnessing it thru',
That when I say *'I do'*, I give my love to you.
As husband and wife, our life is re-born.
Life's turmoils, becoming easier.
We'll be together each morn'.

I know we're not the first.
So others, do know.
The feelings I have are deep,
Continuing to grow.

I'm happy, I'm glad,
That I'm the chosen one,
for I think so highly of you,
feeling special, because of what you do.

On our Wedding Day,
nearing with each new sun,
To this world,
I will vow, my utmost, commitment to you.

Katherine Sharkey

Thurso Bay

As I walk along the headland on this autumn day
        above the peaceful water, of this, our Thurso Bay,
We must not take for granted, the beauty of our land
        it's something that has come to pass, made by God's own hand.

This miracle that is ours, just within our reach
        of clear crystal waters, beside a sun-kissed beach,
I can hear a tiny whisper, as if the breakers say
        come, enjoy the peace, and watch the children play.

I can see the children skipping, barefoot over the sand
        I thank God for creating this, our special piece of land,
there's enjoyment for the taking, everything for free
        and in my heart I know, it's where I love to be.

My childhood now is past, but my memory is ever clear
        of all the things I loved, and people I held dear,
like the grains of sand I am moved, along by the flowing tide
        in life and death I know, it's here I will abide.

Christine Farquhar

Come

'Come unto Me, all you who are weary and burdened, and I will give you rest.' Matthew 11.28

Come unto Me all who are weary
and carry heavy loads,
And I will give you rest.

Come unto Me all who are hungry
and thirsty for the right,
And I will refresh you.

Come unto Me all who are broken
in heart and spirit,
And I will heal you.

Come unto Me, come unto Me,
all in prison to addiction,
And I will set you free.

Come unto Me all who are grieving
and in mourning,
And I will comfort you.

Come unto Me little children,
and I will take you
In My arms and bless you.

Come unto Me all you who are
fatherless, and I will
Be a Father to you.

Come unto Me all who are orphans
and I will never
Leave you nor forsake you.

Come unto Me, come unto Me
all peoples and gather,
Come home to the Father.

O Lamb of God, I come.

Marlene Robbins

The House

Again at dawn, I listen to the house.
The window frames the clouds that veil the moon.
Peat splutters, sweet smell of heather twists and winds through the darkened room
In which I sit
Beside the hearth.

Feelings absorbed within its walls still live.
Welcome and kindness, courtesy are here,
Creaks and cracks, sighs imprisoned long, now drift to me across the years
As I sit
Beside the hearth.

It is a happy house, that clearly shows,
Although it has been torn from end to end,
Piped up and down and round and round and wired to suit my ways, it seems to bear no grudge
To the stranger at its hearth.

The tiny ghost that haunts the house pads soft.
Pressing against my leg, it seems so real.
Its feline face looks up and then it's gone. My own cat, small with fear crouches a chair away,
Still as a mouse
Beside the hearth.

The house can be silent too, it has its moods.
Built to withstand Atlantic gales and storms, its shoulder to the sea.
Its walls and gable ends so thick it shuts the elements away and broods,
A sadness
Beside the hearth.

Although the house is mine in general terms.
Purchased with coin, my name on the Bill of Sale.
I am only its keeper until I leave or die, in trust to maintain its immortality.
I wonder who will follow me, listening
At the hearth.

Eleanor Hamilton

To Clair Gallaher
(Victim blinded in Omagh bombing)

No sympathy can ever reach
The wound that has been made,
On this young innocent life.

No words however grand
Or eloquently conveyed
Can touch the suffering and the loss.

Instead, let joyless, noiseless, tearless
Silence stand, in reverence
Before the cross which has been laid,
Upon this young and blighted form.

Janette Rankin

Remember

Will you remember me
When summer's gone and leaves are falling down
Will you remember me
When snowflakes fall and frost is on the ground
Will you remember me
As years go by and you have moved along
Will you remember
When you hear that old familiar song
Will you remember me
As you lay there in your bed
Will you remember words we whispered
And still hear them in your head
Will you remember me
When you see anothers face
Will you remember
When we shared that last embrace
I remember every word and every smile
Every kiss and every touch
When you were mine a while
I remember it like it was yesterday
Though now it's just a fantasy I play
Forever in my heart my love is true
My darling I remember you.

Eileen Parker

Old Coaching Inn
(Glasgow to Edinburgh road)

A roof that almost touches the ground
and windows of bull's-eye glass.
A door of oak three centuries old
with a knocker of pitted brass.

Walls of stone from a quarry long worked
a seat from a woodland now felled.
While a barrel of many a long year
in ivy's tight embrace is held.

The dust lies decade thick on the floor
covering each table and chair.
As the fire whose welcome's long dead
looks on all with a cold blind stare.

The lanthorn no longer gives comforting light
to the coach coming down the green way.
A horseshoe in a rut is the only token
of a far off, happier and sunnier day.

A traveller in passing at this sad scene
stops and surveys the empty ruination.
Then quickly drives on his way as rain
sweeps over the lonely, cold desolation.

John Bonnar

Daddy

Why, oh why did he let it happen
Why did he let his family go
The children he had fathered
He did not love them so.

Alcohol smote his life
And so it smote us all
Eyes dimmed he could not comprehend
Family life at all.

All through our childhood
Never would he deign
To take pride or pleasure
In our prizes and our gains.

Why, oh why did it happen
He faced death alone
And the family he let go
Not there
When he was called home.

Oh, what a tragic waste
Not only of his life
But the family he let go
Have in their hearts
A twisting knife.

Myra Walker

A Peaceful Nicht?

Some nichts when lying in ma bed
I cannae get tae sleep
Some times it gets sae bad
I start tae count the sheep
But the sheep are no sae very great
Instead o' jumpin' ower the gate
Some wander off aroon' the side
While ithers start tae run and hide
An by the time I've got them sorted oot
I'm wider awake than the owl as it hoots
So by then ma brains intae overdrive
Ma thochts are busier than the bees in a hive
Did a' mind tae switch off the tele?
Did a' mind tae turn off the licht?
Did a' put the cats tae their bed?
Or did a' leave them ootside the nicht?
I really must gie up this smokin'
The money they cost is just a sin
The morra' I'll jist hae ma breakfast
An I'll throw a' ma fags in the bin
I suppose I could hae a read o' ma book
But the batteries in ma torch hiv a run oot
In the name o' God - the alarm's gien me a fricht
As I look oot the windae - I ken see daylicht
Ma bisy thochts must hae sent me tae sleep
Fer I ken fine weel - it wisnae the sheep.

Joyce Melville

This Day, I Make

My morning prayer
two cups of coffee
and a silent word
with thee my Lord

On either side of mid-day
work work work

My evening prayer
a bottle of wine good food
and solemn conversation
interwoven with jest at table with lost and found
friends

And between dusk and dawn
in my deepest chamber
I find myself in you
for a moment ecstatically whole
then in a sudden rush
painfully alone once more

Baria Palka

Fareweel My Dear Scotland
(Perth)

Fareweel my dear Scotland,
I'll love thee for ever.
Fareweel my dear Scotland,
We're bound now tae sever.
I sail for a far land,
Where gold's tae be found,
An' leave thee my Jewel,
Sae cold in the ground!

We met an' were happy,
Seems long, long ago,
Twa youngsters in love,
We would never let go.
But my love and my Jewel,
She now lies alane,
While sae sad an' sae deep,
In my heart lies the pain!

I see her in dreams,
She is here by my side,
I see the wee cottage,
Where we would reside.
I hear her sweet voice
As I picture her there;
Feel the clasp of her hand,
The gold locks of her hair.

So Farewell my dear Scotland,
I'll love thee for ever.
Fareweel my dear Scotland,
We're bound now tae sever.
I sail for a far land,
Where gold's tae be found,
An' leave thee my Jewel,
Sae cold in the ground!

Norrie Sinclair

The Window

A mere green field the crowded woodlands
Into the distance beyond
Golden meadows wheat laden
It could be called a swan's song
The far horizon the hills of Malvern
One can perceive
Oh glorious countryside one has to see it to believe
The trees blow in the windswept sky
Can I think summer is ending and autumn is nigh
As a child I did not appreciate the view from this window
Now of mature years and indeed fate
I am privileged to glance again
And greatly appreciate

Mabel Nickholds

A Welsh Heart

Born in Wales and a mixture of English, Scottish and Irish!
I wonder which country I should hold in my heart.
But as I look out of my windows, I'm certain its Wales.
Trees and fields as far as my eye can see,
Leaves have fallen, before changing colour,
Another window shows Cardigan Bay and the Irish Sea,
Seen from the West Coast.
Further inland spotted on a clear day
By 'diehards' ascending the mountain peaks
That split our land from north to south.
My home, the Llyn Peninsular, my favourite.
My childhood was on a farm by the sea.
Geese, sheep and cows herded by the sheepdogs,
Cats nestled in the byre, contented kittens in the hay,
Lovely, warm milk fresh from the cows,
Chilled before being stored in the waiting churns,
Sheep placidly grazing on sand dunes amid the fields
Or frolicking lambs greeting each spring,
Helpless orphans who were our pets.
My beloved home that I long to recall
Yet realise the changes of the years.
When I visit my mum I can still see the farm
Glancing at it across the bay.
Her home for more than fifty years,
Children born, grown and drifting away.
But, one by one, we all returned here.

T B Smith

Once I Remembered

How I remember that house of so long ago,
Where did the happy, carefree times go?
The long, warm, sunny-shiny days of summer
And winter's coldness of inches of snow.
Sun-baked lizards on smooth, brook stones
Snowmen sentries on boundary walls,
Playmates, young and old, who taught me to see
The beautiful natural world, all around me.
Lonely, only child - not me, for in that extended family
Cosseted and wrapped in love, I lived happily.

Once I remembered the sadness of war,
As a young child, uncomprehending
A mother's tears, a father's grief
For their son, killed on a battlefield.
Men and women working day and night for victory,
Hewing coal, making munitions, composing history,
Sewing and reaping every bit of food from the land
In Home Guard, ARP or Fire Brigade - a happy band.
A whole nation united then for the common good,
Even we little children helped where we could.

Now I remember these scenes from my childhood
With a clarity, enhanced by my advancing years.
In the materialistic world of today, I can attest,
The simplest things in life are truly the best.
Life's hub was the homely farmhouse, spacious for all
Parents, grandparents, uncles and aunts I recall.
Singly, collectively, in memory I see each face,
Sadly, most of them no longer in this earthly place.
Those that are left of the family have grown apart,
But the life of that house, still lives on in my heart.

Gwyne Carnell

True Love

The love in your heart for someone,

The light in their eyes that shines,

The longing to be near that someone,

Until the end of time.

The smile on that face that seeks an embrace,

The closeness that it brings.

The love in your heart for someone,

Is such an eternal thing.

Irene Doris Radford

Temptation

As I travelled along a country lane
    I came across a pretty maid
With auburn hair and big brown eyes
    And a figure that could hypnotise

    I asked her for my way ahead
She did not speak just shook her head
    And pointed to a nearby Inn
Beckoning me with a wicked grin

The thought of what might lay ahead
    A night of passion in a cosy bed
Tempted me I must confess
    For my weary legs in need of rest

    But I carried on my journey's way
    Hoping I wouldn't regret this day
For muggers can be of any size
    And beauty could be just another disguise

John Evans

Spring Offensive

The towpath is like Paschendaele or Mons
After the rain, month after miserable, gurlie
Month of slate-grey skies like battleships. But, once
Again we have come through, survived the hurly-

Burly of Auld Reekie's winter, which did for Fergusson
At twenty-four, and nearly froze the bollocks off Dunbar.
February 2nd - and doubtless premature - today the sun
Sneaked back, a peelie-wally, dimly-remembered star,

Bulldozing winds have gone on one-day strike and calm
Has settled - just for the nonce - on the canal's obscene,
Post-Christmas finery: traffic cones, trolleys, old rubber tyres, a pram,
A plastic blue abandoned sofa, McEwans empties, the polystyrene

Baubles that adorn its face. The faintest touch
Of spring, perhaps, but pairs of water hens, coot couples,
Braces of swans are all already busy on such
Routine recurrent domestic tasks among the ripples

And the reeds as choice of bank, selection of materials and site,
Mooting of plans and foraging for the struts and spars
Of matrimonial homes. Would that the strengthening sun might
Also stir a human blitz, warming the blood of pensioners,

Unemployed youth, TA platoons, pressganged or volunteer
Environmentalists - the hibernating labour force -
Inflaming them with resolution to make spring clean and clear
The waterway for ducks and drakes. Also for all of us, of course.

Norman Bissett

Night Skies

Not many stars shine in our skies at night
Their brilliance dimmed by a myriad of city lights.
Find me a dark place,
A velvet dark place,
There in the hushed silence
The diamond glitter of the sky
Will silver tip the velvet dark place
And outshine the neon glow.

Elizabeth Gwilliam

This Cruel Place

The fiery breath of death has awakened from its slumber like a
vengeful dragon's wrath,
That hangs o'er the battlefield like a spectre that can't control its vile
sanguinary lust.
This cruel place that kills all love must be the devil's path,
Where gentle thoughts are laid to rest to perish in the dust.

This hellish place devoid of love is far from heaven's throne
Yet many men encounter death convinced their blood-stained hands
have touched the shrine of right.
But God has vanished from this place and left us all alone,
For the darkness in our souls has killed God's Holy Love and turned it
into night.

Maurice Cardwell

Star

A friend once said,
Look at the stars in the sky,
Look for the brightest one,
The one up high.

She told me it was you,
Looking down at me,
And when I look up,
Yes, it's you I see.

Damian Begley

No Going Back
(This poem is dedicated to MM)

Death's Heartbreak No More A Flowing Banner.
Ancient Savage At Rest In Stately Manner.

Distant Drums With Their Muffled Beating.
All Kinds Of Voices Pleading, No Retreating.

Where Is The Pain, When People Strive In Pace.
Out Of The Darkness, Face To Face.

Shaken Of Its Shroud, For The Next Generation.
Mindful Of A Darker Day, Born A Nation.

John Leitch

Harshlands

Those distant winds claw near a howling,
The oak trees roar like dogs a growling,
Inside his cottage, paddies scowling
All the kids to wrap up warm.

Yet down the lane old Mary's baking
The lightning strikes as thunder's breaking.
She scurries all the while forsaking,
The outside cry of winter's scorn.

On darkened hills the sheep are crying,
They shelter from the north wind sighing,
In hope of any warmth or drying.
Their sad cries carry on the wind.

The far off household's tillies flicker,
Where elder folk feel older quicker,
As northern winds churn strong and thicker,
As nature breaths a rasping sin.

Ken Watson

Kolinka

Kolinka kolinka kolinka
Yourself you find a way
To dance to a merry tune
No one knows you by moonlight

River flow onward towards Poland
Take away our song Red Army
It was I your witness
Dance dance the night away.

Kolinka kolinka, kolinka kolinka
Yourself take away our troubles
Free us again to dance
Up and away as the River flows

S M Thompson

Dragon Tale

Autumn mornings slow to light
Disperse the darkness of the night
To banish dragons oh so bold
Lock them away and safely hold
Hidden from the children's sight.

Out ran Rachel with all her might
Holding her school bag very tight
Shivering in the crisp foggy cold
Autumn mornings.

She turned to give me a 'fright'
Blowing her breath to her delight
White dragon smoke for me to behold
Almost waiting for the flames to unfold
'Don't be afraid it's only me, alright'
Autumn mornings.

Sarah A P Gallagher

A New Age Dawning

While all newborn innocents
sleep without fear,
the elderly wonder
will they see one more year.

As youths throughout nations
revel in good cheer,
the song 'Auld Lang Syne'
rings out loud and clear.

But here in my country
Northern Ireland its name
candles are burning
a prayer with each flame.

For peace and reconciliation
in the future to last
bigotry and hatred
a thing of the past.

It's time to rebuild lives
in this special new year
for a new age is dawning
now the millennium is here.

Ann Slevin

The Colour Of Despair

Black is black
There is no doubt.
Black is shut
With no way out.

Black is black
Sucking and draining.
Black is bleak
No hope remaining.

Black is cold
And apt to smother.
Black's dark grip
Is like no other.

But black will fade
First pale, then grey.
Black will go
Some bright, white day.

Tanya Fowles

Belfast

Belfast, what do you hold for your children,
For twenty-five years you have stolen
The innocence that should be theirs
For twenty-five years they have used you
As an excuse, a reason.
What happens now, now as they talk and pretend.

Belfast, for all the wrong reasons you are famous,
Worldwide everyone knows what you are,
A child abuser, a murderer, a thief.
Such things are hard to erase
Can you really change?
What is their future?

Karina Dingerkus

Tobacco

I am on my way home,
the days you will be away
loom ahead of me,
my hands are cold and numb in restraint
how distant you are from me now.
The seconds together are a speeding train
the long hours apart a decade in eternity.
I gaze at the horizon,
the soft amber glow warms my heart
my skin is cold,
longing for the warmth of you
how lonely I feel, until I see the grains
the little bark fragments of mortality,
I touch the flesh of my hands and
close my eyes in the imagination
that is your scent.

Lesley P Rainey

Winged Blue

Fragile as a bubble blown
Gentle as a baby's breath
A new seed sown
Winged blue, so frail and pale
From your secret habitat in curled leaf
You emerge, metamorphosis
A miracle of softest blue
You fly
A reflection of the summer sky.

Peggy F Haugh

My Homeland

Beautiful homeland of Ireland, the place I love so well,
Amidst your glorious splendour, I'm content and happy to dwell.
No artist could paint your picture or poets write in rhyme,
No singer could capture the melody, sealed in this heart of mine.

My emerald isle, with its forty shades of green,
Sleepy little leafy glades, with dancing babbling brooks between.
The loftiness of mountains, the billows from your sea,
Land of myth and magic, you mean so much to me.

But mingled with your sweetness, I see your hurt and pain,
I see the scars that marred you, as I hang my head in shame.
I've heard the bombs that ravaged and torn us all apart,
I've seen the weeping Mother, with deep sorrow in her heart.

As the advent of the millennium dawns upon our land,
Embrace each other with friendship, reach out a helping hand.
Heal the pain and suffering, bathe it with our love,
Can't you hear the pleading, our land has had enough.

Eleanor Scott

The Dark

The dark is my only friend.
He surrounds me and comforts me.
I talk to him,
I tell him my worries
my hopes
my dreams
my fears
and I wallow.
The reassuring reply of silence helps me through life,
it gives me strength,
it gives me the courage to fight.

The dark is my cocoon -
I rarely emerge,
it is my safety net,
it catches me when I fall
and wipes my tears away.
For when I leave I wear a mask
which shows no tears
no pain
no suffering
and no truth of who I am.

Nicola Pym

The Cutter

With Forfar in sight I am born in to this world, the first time that
Blue eyes cry tears for my abstinent father in ordered sun sprawled
Sudan
Scotland, a summer myrrh of myrtle, yellowing field, bog, natural
cattle
Work, tar black roads, snares and rabbit carcasses: my young
Mother embroiders spirals to hang at the Fern spore of Newforbank
Little shafts of light that will become the Autumn harvest in time
Simple choices that were woven skilfully in the absence of her
Norman
Cups of golden promise not bitterness, brings a smile to her idealistic
vision of
Heaven

The seeds of change were borne out of this uncertainty, followed by
tumult
Across the north sea, the red sea, deserted on the machir islands
resting place
All by the age of three, I and my family had foundered as individuals,
as family
What we all had embarked upon had now become set out alone and
in life
Grandfather James reflected on this gall as he worked as his task on
an
August day in the thresher. His common task comes out of the need to
Separate the chaff from the corn and distinguish between virtue and
falsehood
His skill, patience, courage and determination were borne out of the
hand that feeds the mouth

I have accepted pain in the physical sense, by today's standard
unburdened self of cuts

How I carried the emotional madness of a corn haired blue-eyed wife in cat/dog days
Suffered the pain of seeing hers, and others weaknesses lead me down the Spiral to
The spirit of our age: dark, love beyond comparison, will I reap the harvest
I have sown through whisky weakness and tobacco trait drenched in polar moods. A
Place further onward and inward, a tiny crevice of light that will allow a blood orange
Harvest in time, a time of giving, a time for enjoyment in song, food, drink, and body
Certainty that growth in the soil will always constitute life, the pattern will continue
Regardless of our fearful human dance

Calum Cumming

My Scotia

Wandering the drought-stricken bushveld, content yet lonely too:
The African sun blazing down on the land; out of a void of blue.
Then I saw the distant mirage, with its trees and loch so cool,
And my thoughts and heart fled homewards to Scotia and Ullapool.

Once again I saw the village, the harbour and the boats at rest,
With dusk settling o'er the water and the sunset pale in the west.
Once more I saw the lights aglow; on the masts of those fishing craft,
And memories sped down the years with the force of a cross-bow shaft.

In fancy I saw those trout aleap; in the rush of a highland stream;
So vivid, so real, so wonderful. O Scotia! How a Scot can dream.
Look there in the brown clear water: is that not a salmon at rest?
Is that not a stag on the hillside, symbol of the land I love best?

In my dreams I saw the mountains; so grim, forbidding and grey,
With the scudding hosts of rain-clouds; where only the eagles play.
The banks of mist now sweeping; all but those peaks from view:
O! Rugged land, O! Wild land, how love for Scotland holds true.

Love for the glens of my forebears, love for the simple and true,
Love for a land that bred courage and such wondrous poetry too.
Love for a land of great principles which also black treachery knew.
Love for Scotia, its peoples, its moorlands and its lochs so blue.

Now that I'm old and weary, with hair bleached white by the sun,
Now that youth has been squandered and I've hung up saddle and gun,
Let me hear the pibroch calling, hear it calling me home once again,
This time to rest forever, beneath North Star, heather and rain.

John H D Robertson

A Millennium View

We stand on the brink of Millennium year,
Past, present and future changes, appear in every sphere.
Man's intervention, technology gear,
Dares to look back over two thousand years.
Advances in Science, education and health
All working together, giving many more wealth.
Despite the progression, great turmoil prevails.
Society's need, and belief that all will be well.
Man looks with dimmed sight, where the Christ-Child was born in a land bleeding and torn;
Making Man's Spirit forlorn.
Yet light beams from afar, earth soaks up it's rays.
We mortals look out excited and dazed,
On the glorious birth of the Millennium age.

Sheila M MacMillan

Millennium

A magical word embracing history
and umpteen mysteries down the ages
our world is full of problems
always has been the case and our own
difficulties and misfortunes
we have to face without wicked stress
Greed is a cancer but what is the answer
the answer we must stop the rot
faithfully care and willingly share
yet we know all these things well enough
so what can be done in two thousand years plus
pray . . . hold fast to The Faith . . . God *is*
Thus - relaxed and refreshed
spread liberally kindness and fun
merry-make celebrate even double-take
our troubles let's bury 'em
and steeped in love - essential
welcome this rare privilege
for a meaningful
Millennium!

Gladys Emily

Nana

I still can't believe
That you are really gone
It has been some time now
Since you were taken from me

I still think of it
Just like it was yesterday
I still see your face, your smile
I still hear your voice, your laughter

I was always scared of dying
Until I saw you go
You looked so happy
To finally be free from pain

Sometimes I wish
I had screamed at you
Or shook you
And told you not to go

But your time was up
You had to go
No matter where you are
Here or there
Forever and ever
I will always love you

Lynne Bissett

Mark Of Decay

Alter of state to what style
Empty space desolate for a while
Decision made in driving haste
Paper office laid to waste
Open land now a lonely place
Disintegration what was now away

In the modern hand of change
Brewing malt falling to small scale
Idle warehouse phantom of illusion
A hole in the region of confusion
Baseless no function open mark
A free for all car park

Things we hold in mind so dear
Come to pass and disappear
Killed by a seed of decay
Commodity didn't make the grade
An empty shell a pile of rubble
A crushing sound to die and fade

Ian Nelson

An Egg-Less Breakfast

It's hard to undo the inherited fate of being born a farmer's son.
Duties of hay and milk and pigs are all enthusiastically done.
Even the eternal smell of manure is a fresh breeze compared to my latest chore.
For the countryside enemy has been at it again.
His beautiful coat in it's roguish red has been dancing in the chicken pen.
Territorial cockerel and maternal hen both slain without remorse.
And for once in my life excitement enters as I imagine our midnight thief.
His eyes and his heart and his tongue and his teeth all pulsing with anticipation,
As he slips through our fence and makes his way to the hut without any complication.
Now breakfasts are cold as my dad eats his egg and sits in silent ponder,
Of his enemy the fox and his property the hens and how to solve this problem he wonders.
But I am his son and he is old so the solution lies with me.
I am nearly a man and the time has come for me to understand,
The rules of warfare, the mark of manhood, as I leave with a gun in my hand.
But the rogue is not my enemy, he has passion just like me and I will not put out the lights of his soul.
So stay clear my friend who brings havoc with him because your life has been placed in my hands.
Avoid bantam baited ambush whose sights are covered and retreat to son-less farms,
Whose duties are performed by un-wished for daughters who would not carry out this command.
I'll sit until dark and wait until light and pray that he will not come.
Oh how it is hard to undo the fate of being born a farmer's son.

D L Ritchie

Invasion Force

Shepherds fall from the sky
Like snow
As they drift
In white silken parachutes.

Each firmly grip their crooks
In their left fists.
Under their left elbows
Each is armed with a sheep.

These are each wrapped in polythene
In case any should, by accident,
Be dropped into the sea.

   Thom Nairn

No One

No one to phone to say you've arrived.
No one to cuddle or curl up beside.
No one to help you on days that are bad.
No one to cry with when thoughts are sad.
No one to laugh with.
No one to hug.
Everyone's busy
There's no one to love.

Wendy Young

A True Freen

When sadness an' worries, an' life's ups an' doons got in ma way,
An' I couldnae see the sunshine fur endless skies o' grey.
It took a true freen tae lift ma spirits up high,
Tae open ma blearie een, an' see the clouds wur passing by.
Fur life wis stairting tae get me jist a wee bit doon.
Ma heid wis fou o' problems, it wis spinning roon an' roon.
But when ma freen helped tae banish awa some o' that fear.
Helped tae mak ma life become a bit mair clear.
Jist wi a bit o' understaunin', time tae listen an' confide.
A true freen helps wi yer emotions, that at times ye canna hide.
Fur a freen is a'body there tomorrow an' throughoot the years,
They niver forsake ye when a difficult moment appears.

Fiona Harvie

About You

I know of a safe place
where I can go
and be neither man nor woman
but be in all its ecstasy
a human being.

Thomas Cunningham

Misplaced Descendants

How many tears did you cry,
From the build up of emotions,
Laid bare from your eyes,
When the memories grow old,
And the stories remain told.
When did you reminisce last,
On the dreams that are jaded,
Obscured by the clouds,
Yet they all seem so faded,
But still relevant it seems,
As of way back when,
The summer had turned,
From the wintery gardens.
When all that was left,
Was a mixed up affair,
A misplaced descendant,
Fading fast from your care,
But you're still covered in dreams,
Conveyed like the skies,
With the sound of thunder,
There was lightning in your eyes,
The shock of surprise,
Did they know you were gone,
Take care of yourself,
Try and find your way home,
Back to your roots,
From pleasures of past,
The restlessness of innocence,
You thought which would last.
Feelings we cherish,
All lost in the game,
While the emotions inside,
Are covered up by the pain,

But the summer will turn,
The weather will open,
Your memories will stay here,
You'll never be forgotten.

Colin Vance

My Dream

I've seen a world that's peaceful
Where children laugh and play,
Fearless as there is no crime
A better world I'd say.

The trees grow tall the flowers bloom
And animals roam free,
Black and white united
It's a sight we all should see.

All races live together here,
No war or terrorists bring fear.
No drought or hunger in this place
No sickness anywhere,
It's beautiful beyond belief
No sight could compare.
One sad thing though it seems,
I find this place only in my dreams.

Jeanie Sterritt

Fort Augustus Abbey, Scotland

Serenity lingers within your proud walls
Now that silence is all that remains.
The memories dance in the halls that once rang
To the sound of a choral refrain.

The beautiful statuary, paintings and books
That furnished you well are now gone,
And are cast on the water of progress to find
Themselves scattered, re-homed and alone.

The sanctuary you gave to so many good souls
Will remain in the ground where you stand,
And the music you made will be borne on the breeze
And carried across this great land.

For some things cannot be destroyed on a whim,
No matter how progress dictates.
So even in silence, you'll hold your head high,
Defying the cruel hand of fate.

Avril Ann Weryk

Millennium 2000
(Oct 16th 1999)

Misty magic curling swirls,
Enticing pretty dancing girls;
Twisting, tapping, twirling, prone,
Chorus girls in millennium dome

Ferris wheel with flickering light,
Science themes to brighten night.
Will we be ready to toast the date?
Are we too early? Should we wait?

The heather is calling and so are the hills,
Rising like monsters from foamy cloud frills.
How can we wait? I see biblical skies
Blazing their fires to cover man's lies.

Scotland brave! Scotland good!
For millennium year we surely should
Celebrate with rare good will:
Let torches burn round every hill.

Imagine now with dreamy eye
This Scottish spectacle on high:
Our strong young men on mountain tops
Counting chimes of striking clocks.

Tramping then in curling snake
Round each hill in figure of eight
With lighted pole and tartan kilt
'Till clocks' last strike - then reigns a lilt.

And as the last strains fade away
The lassies take a turn to play,
Bearing aloft their sparse respite
To guide them home in pale moonlight.

And so with Scottish Traditional Hymn
Let the Millennium be welcomed in.

Marion Gray

Match Day

Each match day in eager anticipation;
I watch the lads run out
Bold and impatient,
Strong and complaisant
Metal studs on concrete chanting
Sounding like hooves of horses cantering,

The whistle blows; The kick is out,
Excited coaches, parents shout -
Heaves and groans, ruck and scrum
Tackles, sprinters, 'Good hands my son'.
Heroes each and every one.

Grass and mud churned up like furrows
Grappling hands of in scrum burrows,
Falling bodies took to the ground
Screams of 'Go on!' A try is bound
Over the line sliding player elated
Whistle blows, a try - a score,
'Keep going lads, we want more'.

A conversion missed, left of the post
A line out called lift and hoist
Hear the trainers sound their voices,
'Ruck it - Ruck it, hold him up,
Pass it out, run like . . . !
Support your player use your men, good hands boys,
Now score again!'

Injured legs and blood replacements
Rain starts falling but still complaisant
Away they go, roaring like lions
The pitch is battered but players unbeaten.

Until the final whistle bays -
A roar goes up of parent's praise
For there's no prouder sport than Rugby in Wales
Where generations experience their parent's tales.

Jacquie Williams

Early Morning

It was early in the morning
When I left my but and ben
Hidden in the shadows
Of a highland glen

The morning air
Was crisp and sharp
As I made my way
On through the dark

The frost was white
Upon the heather
You could hear it crunch
Beneath boots of leather

The moon peeped out
From behind a cloud
Showed the mountain
With its wintry shroud

Now the frost it glistens
Like stars in the night
As it reflected
The moonbeams bright

The sun as it rises
Bringing heat to the day
Melting the frost
With each gentle ray

As each crystal melts
They gather together
And run like teardrops
From each twig of heather

Lex Coghill

Too Late

Had it started when we talked that night,
Or did it just come to light,
This love that lay dormant here in my heart.
The years have gone by and we drifted apart.

We are two different people now,
And I know this love it cannot be.
It has come just too late for you and me.

I cannot forget you, in my life you will still be a part.
Your memory will stay, locked away, in a small secret place
Here in my heart.

Eileen P Dunn

A Country Childhood

At times our childhood seems a world away,
But then again it could be yesterday.
Now from more than sixty years I pen
My memories of life as it was then.

I was born a country child
Through fields my days spent running wild
Or splashing in the dam behind the shed,
Not thinking of a life that lay ahead.
Picking wild strawberries coming home from school,
Or catching 'stickleys' in a shady pool.
Finding a blackbird's nest in a hedge concealed,
Or riding the horses home from the harvest field.
Standing fascinated by the waterwheel
As it caught the rushing torrent, I could feel
The power that threshed the sheaves and crushed the grain.
No child will ever see its like again.
In summer lying in the meadow grass
Listening to the insects as they pass,
Or idly gazing at the bright blue sky,
Making pictures from the clouds that floated by.
Those summer days were long, I'd time to dream
Of fairies dancing by the little stream
That tumbled over stones beside the lane -
I sometimes long to be that child again.
But life waits not for idleness or dreams
Or thoughtful gazing into silver streams.
We have to move on through all the years
Through days of sadness, laughter, joy and tears.

I often live those childhood days again
In memory it was always summer then.

    Sara Huey

Lincolnshire Reveries

As first light on a newborn day
Steals across Lincolnshire fields,
Merlins long stilled echoes whisper,
Warnings of fates now sealed.

Our brightest sons from afar were here,
Their long lost laughter sounds in the wind.
The flights they flew to tyrannous shores,
Battered hard on those iron clad doors.

Not doubting that their cause was right,
Nor counting aught it cost to fight,
When at last their task was done,
Then freedom reigned and chaos gone.

L J Harries

Childhood Days

I remember well, of days gone by,
When, on the rocks, we used to lie,
Catching the sun's rays, from way up high,
Yes, those were the days of childhood.

We knew no fear, when we would jump
From way up high, and land, with a bump,
Spring up again, with a sore rump!
Yes, those were the days of childhood.

We'd climb the hill, at the back o' the ben,
Look out to sea, for the fishermen,
Then play at 'houses', in our den,
Yes, those were the days of childhood.

At half past four, our Mum would call,
We would clamber, over the wall
Put past our toys, coats and ball,
Yes, those were the days of childhood.

After tea, homework, then bed,
Our favourite story, had to be read,
A kiss from Mum, a cuddle with Ted,
Yes, those were the days of childhood.

Evelyne A McMaster

Scotland

Have you ever been to a ceilidh,
Or chased hairy haggis through heather?
Or tasted real Scotch whisky,
Or been drenched by our great Scottish weather?

Have you ever tramped up our mountains,
And admired the wonderful views,
Or tasted a sweet, country pancake,
Left by considerate coos?

Have you ever been kissed by our midges,
Or tickled by thistles at night?
Have you ever seen Nessie in summer -
If you did, did she give you a fright?

Have you ever tried tossing the caber,
Or dancing the Highland Fling?
Or wearing the kilt in deep winter,
With under it, not a thing?

If you've never experienced the pleasure,
Of Alba, our beautiful land,
Come north of the border, you'll love it,
I promise, our country's just grand!

Ivy Burns

Teenage Memories

When I was in my later teens
There wisnae such thing as wearing jeans
Ye dressed yourself in Sunday best
In a three piece suit and silken vest

The suit was worn at church on Sunday
But put away afore reaching Monday
If a dance wis oen I wore the suit
And my pal wore his as well, nae doot

It always happened when we danced aroon
The lassies seemed impressed
Wis it because our curly hair wis broon
Or wis it the way we always dressed

Don't think I depended oen this suit
I had anither yin as well
I had it oen tae work and each day when going' oot
Although it wisnae swell

Both suits got tattered and torn somehow
And dumped away in the past
I've anither new suit oen me now
Hoping it won't be the last

   S T Jennings

The Sixteen Angels Of Dunblane

Who can forget that vile day when the evil reaper stalked,
depraved, inhuman to the core, amongst the innocents walked.
With icy stare he stood there, and for a moment surveyed,
An eerie silence befell the gym, where the innocents had played.

Within minutes lives were shattered, as sixteen angels were gunned down,
and heartache, grief and anguish, soon swept through Dunblane Town.
Each anniversary will take its toll, each birthday, each tomorrow,
And toys with happy memories, put away with heartfelt sorrow.

Each memory will be treasured, each photograph held with pain,
each family will remember, the sixteen angels of Dunblane.
Each holiday will have its memory of each walk upon the shore,
And each parent will remember, of walks and times before.

Each tiny life was not fulfilled which adds to grief and pain,
a senseless act - but not of God - brought sadness to Dunblane.
Each Christmas will never be the same as those families bravely sigh,
But there'll be sixteen little angels singing carols from on High.

For Sophie, David, Megan, John, Emily, Brett, Joanna,
And Emma, Kevin, Charlotte, Ross, Melissa and little Hannah.
Victoria, Abigail and Mhairi, not forgetting teacher Gwen,
Taken from us in an instant, of madness and mayhem.

Ian L Fyfe

Untitled

In the highly competitiveness of our race and realistically
It's a race - we're all wanting to be 'winners' -
Impossible because simply when we're winners we're also losers
The two are interwoven and can't be separated.
I see ambition in us people -
Are fine qualities to be held on to
The striving for excellences or innovation and so on
And looking for improvement to the work at hand.
Here's a quotation worth noting
'None of us are a genius in all things - but all of us have some qualities to offer.
Even the down at heel lonely figure on the streets.

James Callaghan

A Childhood Summer

I remember summer when I was just a lad
Of days that were never ending
The best days I ever had
When the sun rose every morning
And shone till late at night
When school was just a memory
And everything was just right
The games we played together
Hide and seek and kick the can
The days when we went fishing
And got ourselves a tan
Yes! I remember summer
When the wheat and corn were high
And the corncrake in the meadows
Gave it's piercing grating cry
The days of boys together
With not a girl in sight
The days of joy and laughter
When we played with all our might
Oh! How I remember summer
And wished it would never end
But alas I've just been dreaming
And it's all just been pretend
For now it looks like winter
And seems to last all year
Or is it that I feel older
Now that Father Time creeps near

James (Hamish) Seton

Never Say My Dancing Days Are Done

I'm a wee thing short o' breath these days
An' ma pow is gettin' grey,
But the music o' a liltin' tune
Can mak' me jump an' sway.
No' just sae jimp at the jivin' noo,
But ma hert's still fu' o' fun -
Never say ma dancin' days are done!

Be it Scottish country dancin' or live calypso beat,
The toes begin tae twinkle an' there's rhythm in ma feet.
I birl, an' twirl an' gently swirl
An' chassée nice an' neat -
No, never say ma dancin' days are done!

Let's have a worldwide 'dance-in'
Where we're all sae busy prancin'
That we havenae time tae fight or go tae war
Let's have dancin' in the street,
Wi' the polis 'on the beat'.
Never say oor dancin' days are done!

    Margaret M Osoba

My Guilt Is Hurt Enough!

Acts that rule the rich and fool
Laid down in time long gone
Argued still to punish ill
And crime is never done!

The rich they ruled to punish all
To keep the lowest low
In transports hulks or prison rots
The victim of life's blows!

No rules are changed, just rearranged
By tinpot despots still
Protect the strong and stuff the weak
Establishment's the will!

And *justice* moves by little slaves
Depends on who you are
The vandal's laws ignore the case
For lawyers called to bar!

Man's was the will, and ever now
We make the wrongs look right
To punish ill, ignoring still
Humanities true fight!

No Gods nor laws alter the case
Once done the blow is struck
To put things well we cannot tell
Till cause is changed by luck

You'll tell your lies as I despise
Your right my wrong prolongs
I too can judge and never budge
My *guilt* is hurt enough??

    Mike Morrison

The Folk Weekend

When,
>The faithful in Patchouled motley
>Fired by embers of pallid sky.
>Through the mists of beer and roll-ups
>Once again begin to cry.

Then,
>Eye deep in a ring
>Holding hands begin to sing.
>Now the dance is round the phallus
>Every cup a foaming chalice
>Until they all fall down.

Paul Keegan

The Uninvited Guest

Everything it seems is fast asleep
as the mist rolls across the Firth,
bringing the horizon to our feet.

An uninvited guest, a silent stranger.
Mist, as with life, is like a vapour:
It appears for a time
then vanishes away.

An eerie silence hovers
over river, hill and town.
Dawn is breaking chimes the clock,
but time is of no essence
for the mist to take stock.

It seems forever and a day
before daylight breaks our way,
as the mist spreads its mantle,
covering the early morning dew.

Then the vale of silence is rent in two
as the piercing fog-horn blares.
Its sound is coarse,
but a sound that cares.

Birds join in their dawn chorus.
Traffic rises to the bait
as people go about their business,
rushing, rushing to avoid being late.

The uninvited guest is leaving
as quietly as he came.
Leaving behind the same old
hustle and bustle
of our topsy-turvy world,
for which, he is not to blame.

J Henderson Lightbody

Someone Sings The Blues

Tail-to-tail
Tourists
Revellers
Trinket sellers
Screeching brats
Good ol' USA grannies
Shouting in loud checks

Pan pipes
Bag pipes
Precocious violin players
Would-be Bob Dylans

kissy-kiss lovers
Eating each other

Polis beating the beat

Italians meeting in
Cheek to cheek greetings

Camera crews
Filming
Fringe
fools

Teutonic boy scout packs
Healthy Norwegians in plastic macs
Crumpled linen critics
Clown costumed mimics

At one o'clock the gun blows
Someone sings the blues

Jules A Riley

Today

It's the start of a new day
God has been kind
He has given me rest
For my body and mind
So now I'm refreshed
And ready to start
With a spring in my step
And love in my heart
I don't know what lies ahead today
But I'll face it all come what may
Life can be a struggle
Of that I won't deny
Persevere and keep going
The bad times will pass by
Just be the best that you can be
We don't always get it right
It helps to begin your day with God
And end with Him at night.

W Barrett

Untitled

I canna complain it widna be richt
For I wis born wi the gift of sicht
I shouldna moan of my fear
For I wis lucky enough to hear
I've never hid tae thirst or sterv o' breid
I've hid a better life than mony hae heid
And when I close for the last time these eyelids
I ken my greatest present wis ma kids

Rita Rae

Dissolution

She gave him a love, which distilled into his every need.
He only saw the wife, never the woman,
And so, at last, in desolation, she left.

Greta Carty

Love

Love is such a small word
But means so very much

Everyone's meaning of love
Is different
For it takes all sorts of people
To make the world the place it is

For love is special to me to
Show someone love is a gift
You can show it in so many
Ways
By giving flowers or by doing
Things for the ones you love

Or simply feeling someone's loss as
If it was your own

>Money can't buy love
>But you can feel it
>And see it

Love is a gift
For the ones
I love the most my family and dear friends

>*Kirsty Keane*

Life

Life is for living
Life is for giving
Life is to know
Life is to grow
Life is for the seeds that we will sow
Life is for the tears that may flow
Life is for the joys, we would have missed
Were we not alive, did we not exist.

Marguerita J Johnstone

The Artist's Brush

Each of us is an Artist within our own right,
All we need is to imagine to bring it to sight,
The Canvas is waiting the brush is at hand,
And a Rainbow of colour for our mind to expand.

For the picture we paint is within our own mind,
An explosion of colour of no other kind,
And all we need do is just visualise,
For the colour to be there within your mind's eye.

So let's pick up the brush without any delay,
And see for yourself how your colours display,
Some maybe bright whilst other seem grey,
A mixture of emotions felt in one day.

Your colours may dance they might even sing,
Bring wonderful joy like the first breath of spring,
They may reach out and touch you as if to endear,
That you awaken to compassion with one single tear.

As you continue to paint with each stroke of the brush,
Be aware of the silence the calming the hush,
A stillness a peace eternally flowing,
A love beyond words that's forever ongoing.

The colours can bring all this and more,
Right there at your fingertips for you to explore,
A lifetime of discovery no need to rush,
After all . . . You are the Artist . . . and your hand holds the brush.

Elizabeth C Craig

Michaelmas Bucolic

Season of beauty, with poignant flavescence,
Tinging and ageing the radiant green;
Nature enhanced with maturing senescence,
Painting a Constable countryside scene.

V skeins of Brent geese, from boreal breeding,
Winging their way to a recognised strand;
Guiding his gaggle. Experience leading,
Breaking formation while wheeling to land.

Harsh murmuration of starlings contending
Building of rooks raucous claim to their trees;
Transient ducks, line astern, slowly wending
An austral alignment, to goal overseas.

Daylight abridged by a lengthening darkness,
Shading extinction in soft lunar beam.
Soon all my world will display a bleak starkness;
Winter's dictatorship reigning supreme.

Alasdair Maciver

Pharoah's Wife

In the Egyptian Room, behind glass,
the jewels of a queen.

Here are her necklaces:
the dove-grey of faience beads,
the bottle-green of amazonites,
the waxy-blue of chalcedony.
See how her head-dresses glow
with carnelians and amethysts,
crafted to complement her skin!

There are her rings, set with garnets
crimson as gouts of blood;
and for her arms, bracelets: of gold,
silver, and honey-coloured electrum.
Can't you just picture the eyelids,
black with kohl, that deadly antimony?

Will he come tonight? Say he will come!
The gateman is bribed; was it enough?
The boy-king sleeps in his chamber:
I put poppy-syrup in his wine,
my hand-maidens will say nothing.
And now, the waiting. O, say he will come!

I have bathed. I have anointed my body
with the scented oil from Cathay,
painted my eyelids with the black mystery.
I am ready; soon, soon he will come,
his sandals treading softly in the dust.

Will he like my necklace,
my rings, my bracelets?
How my thighs ache for him!

    Ken Angus

Camp 1950

School camp was great fun
It seemed to be just the trick
But a lot missed their mum
Many obviously were homesick
Still the best was done
To excite us and enjoy
Growing up, we've not to cry
Get on and enjoy the break
All that has been planned
Doing your best for parents' sake
Leaders are there to give a hand
The week will soon be o'er
Too soon we'll be going home
Just when you're wishing
There would be much more.

William Easton